What Really Matters in Fluency

Research-Based Practices across the Curriculum

Richard L. Allington

University of Tennessee, Knoxville

Boston • New York • San Francisco
Mexico City • Montreal • Toronto • London • Madrid • Munich • Paris
Hong Kong • Singapore • Tokyo • Cape Town • Sydney

Executive Editor: Aurora Martínez Ramos
Series Editorial Assistant: Kara Kikel
Marketing Manager: Danae April
Production Editor: Annette Joseph
Editorial Production Service: Lynda Griffiths
Composition Buyer: Linda Cox
Manufacturing Buyer: Linda Morris
Electronic Composition: Denise Hoffman
Interior Design: Denise Hoffman
Cover Designer: Kristina Mose-Libon

For Professional Development resources, visit www.allynbaconmerrill.com.

Between the time website information is gathered and then published, it is not unusual for some sites to have closed. Also, the transcription of URLs can result in typographical errors. The publisher would appreciate notification where these errors occur so that they may be corrected in subsequent editions.

ISBN-10: 0-205-57058-5
ISBN-13: 978-0-205-57058-4

Printed in the United States of America

10 9 8 7 6 5 4 3 BRR 12 11 10 09

**Allyn & Bacon
is an imprint of**

PEARSON

www.pearsonhighered.com

Contents

chapter 6

Interventions to Foster Fluency Development in Struggling Readers   91

Preface

Reading fluency has become a hot topic primarily because of the 2000 report of the National Reading Panel. Although fluency is an important component of reading development, I worry that it is not well understood. Because it is unclear to some educators, it is too common that misguided instructional efforts are observed in the name of improving fluency.

In this book I provide a plain-language discussion of the notion of fluency, cite research on fluency assessment and fluency development, and offer clear guidelines for promoting development of reading fluency. I begin by describing what is known about fluency development and the assessment of fluency, while also noting that it takes time for fluency to develop in beginning readers. I then discuss how reading speed and fluency are two related but different proficiencies and why many currently popular assessments of fluency confuse speed with fluency. Finally, I discuss how fluency can be best fostered in classroom reading lessons and in intervention programs for children who struggle with reading acquisition.

In the end, I argue, dsyfluent reading is more often instructionally induced than caused by problems inherent in the student. Teachers can ease beginning readers' transitions from word callers to fluent readers and they can accelerate the development of fluency in struggling readers, but they must get classroom reading and intervention lessons just right to accomplish this. My hope is that after completing this book you will have the knowledge and skill needed to do both.

Thank you to the following reviewers for their comments and suggestions: Mary DeKonty Applegate, St. Joseph's University; Kristy Dunlap, George Mason University; and Pamela Williamson, University of Cincinnati, CECH; and to Lisa Wiedmann, Rhinelander Public Schools, WI, for providing the Study Guide.

The **What Really Matters** *Series*

The past decade or so has seen a dramatic increase in the interest in what the research says about reading instruction. Much of this interest was stimulated by several recent federal education programs: the Reading Excellence Act of 1998, the No Child Left Behind Act of 2001, and the Individuals with Disabilities Education Act of 2004. The commonality shared by each of these federal laws is that each restricts the use of federal funds except for instructional services and support that had been found to be effective through "scientific research."

In this new series we bring you the best research-based instructional advice available. In addition, we have cut through the research jargon and at least some of the messiness and provide plain-language guides for teaching students to read. Our focus is helping you use the research as you plan and deliver reading lessons to your students. Our goal is that your lessons be as effective as we know how, given the research that has been published.

Our aim is that all children become active and engaged readers and that all develop the proficiencies needed to be strong independent readers. For us, strong independent readers are active and comprehending readers. Each of the short books in this series features what we know about one aspect of teaching and learning to read independently with understanding. Each of these pieces is important to this goal but none is more important than the ultimate goal: active, strong, independent readers who read with understanding.

So, enjoy these books and teach them all to read.

chapter 1

What Is Fluency and Why Is It "Hot"?

Fluency activities are common today, especially in the early elementary grades and for struggling readers at all grade levels. But what exactly does *fluency* mean, and why is it "hot" all of a sudden? In this chapter, you will find answers to both parts of the question.

⭐ What Is Fluency?

There are at least three notions of *fluency* that are currently used:

- Fluency is reading aloud with accuracy, appropriate speed, and expression. This is the oldest (Huey, 1908/1968, p. 140) and most common definition.

- Fluency is reading accurately while also comprehending what is read (LaBerge & Samuels, 1974). This is also a historical definition tied to "automaticity theory."

- Fluency is reading aloud fast and accurately. This is a recent definition (Good & Kaminski, 2002), one at odds with both historical definitions because neither "expression" nor "comprehension" is typically evaluated in calculating a student's fluency performance.

Each of these definitions is discussed in some detail and the instructional implications of each definition are considered.

Fluency as Reading Aloud with Accuracy, Appropriate Speed, and Expression

As children begin to learn to read, word-by-word reading is the norm (Chall, 1983). In fact, this sort of reading may be essential as children begin to figure out the concept of "word." Along with the word-by-word reading comes "finger-point reading" where children track their reading with their fingers. The word-by-word reading is almost necessarily monotonic. That is, there is little inflection or change of pitch. The word-by-word reading sounds almost as if the child were reading from a list of words.

Over time, the typical beginning reader begins to read in phrases and stops pointing to each word. Classroom teachers begin to observe the initiation of what they usually think of when they say "fluent" reading. It means that readers are now reading aloud with expression. In this case, "expression" is observed when readers modulate their voices and pause appropriately at phrase boundaries and at the end of sentences (Huey, 1908/1968). In other words, the readers "sound good" when reading aloud.

This historical definition of fluent reading is captured in the phrase "reading with expression." Perhaps the historical aspect of this definition stems from the earlier tradition of teaching reading more along the lines of rhetoric than anything else. That is, until the 1920s, reading instruction in much of the English-speaking world had good oral reading as an end goal. But between 1900 and 1920, leading literacy scholars vigorously challenged this dominant view. They argued that reading with understanding, especially silent reading comprehension, should be the end goal of reading instruction. They provided good evidence that many students could easily and accurately read aloud the words on a page but with little understanding of what they had read (Smith, 1934). The experts argued for substantially modifying the role of reading aloud during instruction and even published the first books for teachers on how to foster silent reading comprehension (Smith, 1925).

In a short period of time the focus of reading instruction shifted and the emphasis on expressive oral reading was largely lost from lesson plans and teachers' guides that accompanied the reading series. Nonetheless, classroom teachers continued to notice when a child's reading was not fluent, although there were few guidelines for assessing or enhancing the fluency of those children.

Fluency as Reading Accurately While Also Comprehending What Is Read

This notion of fluency derives from automaticity theory (LaBerge & Samuels, 1974). That theory argued that when decoding difficulties used too much cognitive capacity, comprehension would be unlikely because there would be little attentional space left for using comprehension processes. Beginning readers, the theorists argued, use lots of cognitive capacity just to read the words. As their decoding and word recognition develop, less capacity is needed to recognize words, and therefore cognitive space is available for comprehension to occur. In this theoretical model, fluent reading was defined as reading where word recognition was largely "automatic," using little cognitive attention, and thus comprehension was possible. As Samuels (2006) recently noted, "To be considered a fluent reader, the person should be able to decode and comprehend at the same time" (p. 340).

Fluency, under this definition, is actually the ability to do at least two things at once, decode and comprehend. Samuels (2007) has critiqued current fluency assessments (e.g., Dynamic Indicators of Basic Early Literacy Skills, or DIBELS) for their failure to include reliable estimates of comprehension in evaluating fluency.

Fluency as Reading Aloud Fast and Accurately

Fluency as reading fast and accurately is the more recent, and contested, definition. This version of fluency has been promoted by the developers of the DIBELS assessment package and has gained a foothold in many schools, especially schools participating in the federal Reading First program under the No Child Left Behind Act (NCLB). There have been sharp criticisms of this definition and this assessment package (e.g., Goodman, 2006; Mathson, Solic, & Allington, 2006; Pressley, Hilden, & Shanklin, 2005; Samuels, 2007), but those critiques will be discussed in detail in Chapter 4.

The criticisms fall under two broad themes. First is the question of whether the widespread use of DIBELS in Reading First schools is the result of the assessment's merits or an example of crony capitalism. That is, the Inspector General of the U.S. Department of Education investigated the use of DIBELS in Reading First schools and reported evidence of coercion by federal officials in the selection of monitoring tools (Office of the Inspector General, 2006). The second set of criticisms primarily relate to technical qualities of the DIBELS assessment package (Pressley, Hilden, & Shanklin, 2005).

DIBELS provides several skills assessments (letter-name fluency, non-word reading, oral reading of short passages) and reports all scores as fluency scores (e.g., letter-naming fluency). However, DIBELS is simply a rate assessment, not a fluency assessment. What one learns from DIBELS is how fast children can name letters and read words, non-words, or passages aloud. Such assessments are more automaticity assessments than fluency assessments, at least given the historical understanding of what reading fluency means.

As Samuels (2007) concludes, "One criticism I have of the DIBELS tests is that, despite their labels, they are not valid tests of the construct of fluency as it is widely understood and defined. They only assess accuracy and speed. The creators of DIBELS are guilty of reification. By attaching the term *fluency* to their tests, they create the false assumption that that is what their tests measure."

Summary   From this point, I will write of fluency using the historical definition of "reading aloud accurately with expression." I will also suggest that,
given the evidence that some children can read accurately and fast while
comprehending little, educators must also pay attention to the second definition and incorporate measures of comprehension into their assessments of
fluency development and their instruction.

☆ Fluency Hits the Big Time

Twenty-five years ago I wrote an article (Allington, 1983a) titled "Fluency:
The Neglected Goal." In that paper I bemoaned the fact that so many struggling readers were more likely to read word-by-word than read in phrases.
They were also more likely, I wrote, to read in a flat monotone rather than
read with expression. I argued that for these children, reading was a laborious
process and that reading, for them, could hardly be pleasurable or meaningful. In this review of the research that existed on fluency I suggested that
helping these struggling readers develop more fluent reading should be a
more common instructional goal.

There was a decade-long (1980–1990) flurry of activity around that
notion, primarily studies investigating the usefulness of an instructional
routine known as "repeated readings" (Samuels, 1979). But in the following
decade (1990–2000) fluency largely vanished from both the research and
the instructional scenes.

In 2000, the National Reading Panel (NRP) released its report, *Teaching
Children to Read: An Evidence-Based Assessment of the Scientific Research Literature
on Reading and Its Implications for Reading Instruction,* and named fluency as one
of the five pillars of "scientific" reading instruction. Suddenly, fluency was,
once again, "hot." Today in schools, fluency is one focus of early reading
lessons (and a focus of lessons for older struggling readers), and in many
schools fluency development is being monitored. In fact, in some schools, for
some readers, fluency development is a major instructional goal.

I worry, however, that fluency is not well understood and, because of that,
much of the focus on fluency development is misguided at best. Thus, in this
small book I hope to clarify what experts know about fluency, its assessment,

and development. I hope that the information provided helps educators place an appropriate emphasis on fluency and helps identify appropriate assessment and instructional activities for monitoring fluency development.

⭐ Why Is Fluency Important?

Focusing on fluency, reading aloud accurately with expression and comprehension, has been named one of the five pillars of scientific reading instruction. But just what evidence did the NRP consider before identifying fluency as an important aspect of reading development and an important instructional goal? In the section that follows, I will review the NRP findings and other theories and research that support the current emphasis on fluency. I will also note that there is much about fluency that is not well understood.

Fluency and the NRP

The NRP noted that the large-scale national study of fluency and comprehension conducted by Pinnell and others (1995) had found a "close relationship" between the two proficiencies. That is, in this study, the fourth-grade students who exhibited poor fluency also exhibited poor comprehension. Pinnell and colleagues measured fluency on a four-point scale that included "expression" in the ratings (see Figure 4.3 in Chapter 4 for the fluency scale they used).

In addition, the National Research Council had earlier concluded, "Adequate progress in learning to read English (or any alphabetic language) beyond the initial level depends on sufficient practice in reading to achieve fluency with different texts" (Snow, Burns, & Griffin, 1998, p. 223). Given these findings, the National Reading Panel decided to examine the research on fluency and the relationship of fluency to reading development.

The NRP located experimental studies that studied the effects of guided oral reading practice on reading fluency and other reading proficiencies. In these studies, the NRP included those that employed a variety of practices, including repeated reading, paired reading, shared reading, and assisted reading. In the end, the NRP conducted a meta-analysis on 77 research reports published since 1990 that met their stringent criteria.

Unfortunately, only 14 of the 77 studies provided sufficient data to be used in the meta-analysis the NRP conducted. In 12 of these 14 studies, positive effects for a variety of guided reading procedures were reported. In 2 studies, no significant differences were found between the groups participating in a guided reading activity and groups not participating. For these 14 studies, the NRP reported generally small effect sizes ($d = .50$ on general reading achievement, .55 on reading accuracy, .44 on fluency, and .35 on comprehension). Thus, the panel concluded that engaging students in a variety of guided oral activities produced a small improvement in students' reading proficiencies. However, the largest effect size was for accuracy of reading words only in the passages that students practiced. The smallest effect was on students' reading comprehension. The NRP findings showed that guided reading practice had the largest effects on word recognition, reading speed, and oral reading accuracy and a smaller effect on comprehension.

Finally, the majority of the studies focused on developing fluency in struggling readers, with only five studies including normally developing readers. Thus, the research available seems more supportive of using guided reading procedures with poor readers, with less evidence available on the use of these strategies for most pupils.

Meta-analysis is a statistical technique for examining the effects of a treatment across multiple studies. It is an improvement over using simple statistical significance because statistical significance reveals only the likelihood that the results could have occurred by chance. In other words, when you see that an experiment found a $p = <.05$ level of statistical significance, that means that if the experiment were replicated 100 times you could expect that you would get the same findings in 95 of the experiments but different results in the remaining 5 experiments. Meta-analysis results in effect sizes in addition to statistical significance. The effect size calculation is an attempt to answer the question: How much of a difference did the experimental treatment make? Effect sizes of 0 to .25 are considered trivial, .25 to .50 small, .50 to .75 moderate, and effects sizes larger than .75 are considered large.

The NRP then concluded that guided oral reading practice was, in fact, important in the development of reading fluency and that reading fluency was important in the development of general reading abilities. However, the NRP also said that there were many questions left unanswered in the research on guided reading practice and fluency development:

> Research is needed to disentangle the particular contributions of components of guided reading, such as oral reading, guidance, repetition, and text factors. And it is important to know for which children, at what level of reading ability and in what setting and by whom (teachers, classroom aides, peers, parents) and for how long do different approaches to guided oral reading work best? Research is needed over longer time spans to provide information about the emergence of fluency and its relationship to specific instructional practices. (National Reading Panel, 2000, pp. 3–4)

In other words, research generally indicates the benefits of guided reading practice for fluency development and the general relationship between fluency development and the development of broader reading proficiencies. What is not well understood is just what specific instructional factors are most essential in explaining these relationships.

Sustained Silent Reading

In the same section on fluency, the NRP also examined the research on silent reading practice for effects on reading achievement. Here, they located studies primarily of sustained silent reading (SSR). Included were studies of Drop Everything and Read (DEAR), uninterrupted sustained silent reading (USSR), and the Accelerated Reader commercial program. The NRP located only 14 studies that met their criteria for analysis. Unfortunately, none of these studies was actually very well designed to answer the question of the effects of independent silent reading practice on fluency or other reading proficiencies. First, none measured whether the intervention actually increased the volume of reading done by the participating students. Second, many of the studies were of a short duration (e.g., 3 to 6 weeks in length). Because of the small number of studies, the NRP did not conduct a meta-analysis on the 14 studies but rather simply analyzed each one for the presence of positive effects on some aspect of reading achievement. The panel reported that the majority of the studies it reviewed did not find positive effects for sustained silent reading activities.

However, the NRP also noted that when comparing sustained silent reading activities to other instructional activities, the finding of no significant difference suggested that sustained silent reading worked at least as well as engaging pupils in the sorts of lesson activities typically found in classrooms. But the NRP (2001) then argued, "That encouraging more reading does as well as certain instructional activities in stimulating learning does not speak well of those instructional activities. Voluntary reading within the school day should be compared against non-reading activities or activities in which the amount of reading can be carefully measured" (pp. 3–27).

National Reading Panel member S. Jay Samuels (2002) noted, "Having advocated extensive reading as a way to increase fluency, in fairness, I should point out that the fluency section of the NRP report neither endorses nor condemns independent silent reading. Failure to endorse should not be interpreted as a criticism of this technique, however" (2002, p. 174).

In commenting on the controversy the NRP created, panel member Tim Shanahan (2002) stated:

> What the panel did study was the efficacy of various procedures and programs used to encourage children to read more. The issue that the NRP studied was not whether independent reading had value, but what school efforts led children to increase their amount of reading. The NRP examined the research on procedures like SSR and DEAR, which set aside time within the school day for free reading, commercial programs aimed at encouraging more reading, and various incentive plans.
>
> The conclusion: None of these programs or procedures has proven it effectively gets students to read more and, consequently, to read better. The NRP did not reject the possibility that some procedures might succeed in encouraging reading, and it called for more research on the issue. . . . No matter what the benefits of reading—and they appear extensive—not all plans for encouraging kids to read more are likely to work. Schools should be cautious about adopting such uncharted schemes on a large scale. (p. 38)

Both the NRP report and these comments from two NRP members suggest that few well-designed studies of the effect of volume of reading activity are available, but none suggest having no role for reading volume in the development of reading proficiencies.

In a broadly disseminated guide for teachers, the National Institute for Literacy (NIFL) seemed to ignore the NRP findings: "Rather than allocating instructional time for independent reading in the classroom, encourage your students to read more outside of school" (Armbruster, Lehr, & Osborn, 2001, p. 29). This advice to banish in-school independent reading and to have pupils read more after school is a misrepresentation of the NRP findings and it is also bad advice. This is because struggling readers, the students most in need of independent reading, simply do not do it outside of school (Anderson, Wilson, & Fielding, 1988).

Although this advice was said to have been drawn from the NRP findings, it obviously is not and, in fact, includes a puzzling recommendation in suggesting that there is evidence that indicates that independent reading outside of school is causally related to reading achievement, but no evidence supports such reading during the school day. According to NRP member Samuels (2006), there is nothing in the NRP report that would suggest evidence for this position.

Additionally, researcher Steven Krashen (2004) noted that the NRP failed to locate a number of studies of sustained silent reading that he had identified. He reported that 8 of the 10 studies of sustained silent reading that lasted one school year or longer produced positive effects on reading achievement, with the remaining 2 studies reporting no difference in student performance between the treatment and control groups. A major criticism of the NRP analysis leveled by Krashen was that shorter-term studies (as short as 10 weeks) of sustained silent reading dominated the pool of studies the panel reviewed. Expecting measurable improvements in reading in such a short time period is expecting a lot.

Finally, the National Research Council reached the opposite conclusion from the NRP after reviewing the research on independent reading:

> Throughout the early grades, time, materials, and resources should be provided (a) to support daily independent reading of texts selected to be of particular interest for the individual student, and also beneath the individual student's frustration level, in order to consolidate the student's capacity for independent reading and (b) to support daily assisted or supported reading and rereading of texts that are slightly more difficult in wording or in linguistic, rhetorical, or conceptual structure in order to promote advances in the student's capacities. (Snow, Burns, & Griffin, 1998, p. 234)

Thus, the question of the role of independent reading in the development of fluency and other reading proficiencies remains contested, with the NIFL stance that it should be excluded from school reading activities—the most negative, and most obviously incorrect, interpretation of what the research says.

What the Research Says about the Role of Reading Volume in Fostering Fluency

As the NRP pointed out, there are actually only a small number of experimental studies of the impact of increasing the volume of independent reading that pupils do. And there are even fewer well-designed, longer-term studies. But there are, literally, hundreds of correlational studies demonstrating that better readers read more than weaker readers.

The most common correlational studies simply compare the volume of reading observed or reported by good and poor readers and then correlate the volume with the students' reading achievement. In such studies the results point to a universally accepted conclusion. Good readers do read more than poor readers, both in school and at home. That is, they are assigned more reading activity by their teachers during the school day and they voluntarily read more when they are out of school. In an early study I conducted, for instance, a first-grade good reader read 1,933 words during his weekly reading lessons, whereas a poor first-grade reader in the same classroom read only 16 words (Allington, 1984). The poor reader read very little because his lessons focused on round-robin oral reading of only a sentence or two every other day, but the lessons provided him with lots of skills instruction. The good reader's lessons focused primarily on silent reading of whole stories, not sentences, and on comprehending what he had read.

In this early study I did not manipulate the volume of reading the good and poor readers did. Instead I observed their reading lessons. This is what might be called a "natural experiment" because even though I didn't manipulate the volume of reading, differences did occur in real classroom lessons that were observed. Had I designed an experiment that produced such differences in reading every week and then found that the children who were assigned by me to read very little actually made little progress in reading development, I would have had an experiment and could then use the outcomes to argue for a causal role for reading volume. But because I didn't dictate how much reading these students would do, the results are not considered causal evidence for the role reading volume plays in reading development.

In other words, even though numerous researchers have reported that good readers read more than poor readers (Stanovich, 2000), those studies are not considered strong evidence that reading more produces better reading. However, when correlational studies number in the hundreds, and when each of these studies reports the same relationship between reading volume and reading achievement, it is risky, to say the least, to ignore the findings.

It was those sorts of studies that led me to write "If They Don't Read Much, How They Ever Gonna Get Good?" some 30 years ago (Allington, 1977). Today I will argue that there exists even better evidence for the importance of considering just how reading volume impacts reading achievement. In Chapter 2, I explore just why reading volume is important and how the issue is more complex than many researchers expect. But for now, let me review some of the available evidence that points to just how beneficial increasing the volume of reading can be, especially for struggling readers.

Following the release of the NRP report, Lewis and Samuels (2004) conducted a meta-analysis of 49 studies of reading volume and concluded:

> This review provided support for a moderately strong, positive relationship between reading exposure and reading outcomes. Separate analysis of d-index effect sizes from experimental studies provided clear causal evidence that students who have in-school independent reading time in addition to regular reading instruction, do significantly better on measures of reading achievement than peers who have not had reading time. (p. 1)

In fact, Lewis and Samuels report an effect size of $d = .42$ for reading volume. That d statistic is almost identical to the effect size reported by the NRP for the effect of adding systematic phonics as an instructional feature ($d = .44$). In other words, the authors found that lessons that increased students' volume of reading produced achievement gains of the same size as the NRP reported for lessons including systematic phonics instruction.

There are other research studies indicating that increasing reading volume improves reading proficiencies achievement. Kuhn and Stahl (1998), for

▶ Free, voluntary reading is an essential factor in the development of reading fluency. As McGill-Franzen (1993) noted, series books provide much support and repetition critical to fostering fluency.

instance, in their review of the research on vocabulary acquisition, concluded, "Ultimately, increasing the amount of reading children do seems to be the most reliable approach to improving their knowledge of word meanings, with or without additional training in learning words from context" (pp. 135–136). Oddly, the NIFL document presented the same conclusion about the role of wide reading in fostering vocabulary growth while also recommending against allocating time for students to read independently during the school day.

Finally, Melanie Kuhn and colleagues (2007) have provided new evidence on the importance of reading volume, especially for facilitating fluency development. They compared a repeated reading intervention with a wide reading intervention on fluency development. In these studies, the wide reading intervention produced fluency improvements faster than the repeated reading treatment.

★ Summary

Fluency—accurate, expressive reading—is one aspect of reading proficiency and it seems important for reading comprehension. There are a number of factors related to fluency difficulties, and limited reading activity is one of those factors. Although research illustrates that wide, independent reading contributes to fluency development, there are other aspects of reading instruction that also effect fluency development.

Most beginning readers become fluent readers with little explicit fluency instruction, but some beginning readers never seem to get the hang of it. They read slowly and laboriously even when they are reading with a high degree of accuracy. Other readers also plod along when reading but read less accurately. In the next chapter you will learn how fluency develops normally and why some readers exhibit substantial difficulty in acquiring fluency.

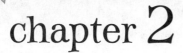

chapter 2

How Is Fluency Normally Developed?

Have you ever observed a young child "pretend" reading—a 3- or 4-year-old child who picks up a book and begins to "read" aloud to you or to another child or a stuffed animal? In most cases, the child has been read that book several times and is now "reading" from memory.

But what is interesting is that the child actually sounds as if he or she *is* reading. By that, I mean the child reads expressively, just like a good reader. In some cases this expressive reading may not even be very accurate, but it does sound like oral reading.

There is a specific voice register that people use when reading aloud. In other words, in almost every case you can tell when someone is talking rather than reading aloud. (The exceptions here are largely confined to polished politicians and news anchors who have become very adept at reading from a teleprompter—they sound like they are talking when they are reading.) Think of it this way. If I played an audiotape recording of a person telling a story and then played a tape of that same person reading from a storybook, wouldn't you recognize which recording was which? Trust me, you would, because reading aloud is a specific speech act with features of its own.

I begin with this information because reading fluently relies on the models of reading aloud that young children hear. When parents, caretakers, and preschool and kindergarten teachers read aloud, they provide models of what fluent oral reading sounds like. The more models a child has, the better. How many models of how many stories are needed to foster easing into fluent reading from the start? No one knows for sure, but it does seem as though children who arrive at school with many, many experiences of being read to almost invariably become fluent readers unless something in the classroom instruction interferes. Some of the details involved in reading fluently are drawn from one's knowledge of speaking conventions (Weber, 2006); it is listening to fluent reading that begins the process of becoming a fluent reader.

No child actually begins the reading acquisition process reading fluently. Jeanne Chall (1983) called an initial phase of reading the "glued to print" stage. At this initial stage children literally read word-by-word. They typically finger-point each word as they read. This "voice-print matching" is a critical phase as children come to understand the concept of "word" and begin to actually attend to the print they are reading. The child mentioned earlier who was engaged in oral "memory reading" of a text can often be observed looking up even while continuing to "read." Eventually, though, children begin to understand that there is a match between the printed page and what you read.

This voice-print connection is one reason to always use a pointer when reading big books aloud to children. Pointing to each word as you read aloud directs children's attention to the print and supports the development of the concept of "word." When people talk, words often run together; and before children begin to pay attention to print, there is no reason they should be able to accurately count the words in a spoken sentence (McGill-Franzen, 2006). It is experiences with print (lap reading where the print is visible, big book read-alouds, language experience stories written on chart paper and then reread) that foster attention to print and printed words. It is through print experiences like these that children come to understand that "gointo" is actually two words: going to. Lots of these experiences help children acquire the ability to finger-point read.

As children then develop and consolidate the initial understandings of how reading is accomplished, the glued-to-print, word-by-word reading is an important step in becoming a "real" reader. Most children begin to move out of the word-by-word phase when reading appropriately difficult material before the end of first grade. Initially, one can observe the use of phrasing and then intonation as children read texts they have read before or that the teacher has read to them. By the end of second grade, most children read grade-level material in phrases and with expression upon their first reading of the material. Children do this with little instructional emphasis on either phrasing or expression. By this, I mean that, historically, there has been little focus on fostering fluency, especially with normally developing readers (Allington, 1983b).

Primary-grade teachers might occasionally mention or model how the voice is supposed to rise when the text being read is a question. Or they might note the rising intonation needed when an exclamation mark ends a sentence. Perhaps at times they will ask a child to reread a sentence if the first reading got the phrasing wrong. They may point out that quotation marks indicate that someone is speaking. Occasionally, children spontaneously reread a sentence when they notice that their phrasing or intonation is wrong. But most often children acquire the ability to read fluently, with phrasing and expression, with little instructional guidance.

Those early experiences of being read aloud to undoubtedly influence this development, but little research exists on just how this occurs. Likewise, while moving from the glued-to-print stage to a phrase-reading stage, children must learn several things about fluent reading that can be derived from their experience as English speakers. Again, there is little empirical research on this, but Rose-Marie Weber, a linguist with a long history of studying beginning reading, has detailed some of the things children might transfer from speaking to reading aloud.

⭐ Function Words

Weber (2006) explains the unique difficulties that function words create for beginning and struggling readers when it comes to reading aloud fluently. First, she notes that function words, such as *of, the, a, do, what, there, when, would, if, for*, and *who*, account for about half of the words that children read. In terms of frequency, the 50 most frequent words that children will see in print are all function words.

Historically, reading researchers have noted the difficulties that children have in learning to recognize function words both when reading from flashcards or a word list and when reading stories. The most common explanations of the difficulties children have with these words have been regarded as stemming from both the meaning (What does *of* mean?) and the graphic similarities (*of, off, if, where, were, there*) of many function words. Weber (2006) notes that these are surely true sources of some of the difficulty because much evidence shows that children learn content words such as *apple* or *car* more quickly than function words such as *of* and *for*. Additionally, children more often confuse visually similar function words when reading lists or stories (e.g., *of/if/off, for/from* and *which/with,* and *where/when* or *were/where/there* confusions).

Weber (2006) argues, however, that there is another aspect of function words that also seems to contribute to their difficulty. That is the fact that function words are typically unstressed in both talk and reading text aloud. Part of what gives English its unique rhythmic quality is the stress on content words and the lack of stress on function words. This lack of stress often creates a pronunciation shift in function words such that the vowel is spoken/read as a schwa. This can be observed in how the word *can* is spoken in the following instances.

I can run fast.	[I'kn run fast.]
You can?	[You can?]
You can go with me.	[You'kn go wid me. Or, You'kn go wif'me.]

In other words, children have difficulty with function words because their pronunciation often shifts depending on what role they play in a sentence.

In addition, in many cases they almost seem as if they were a syllable in an adjoining word (you'kn, wan'na, did'ja, hav'ta) in casual speech and *in fluent reading*.

One key difference, then, between fluent readers and those readers who do not demonstrate fluency is the nature of the pronunciations of function words. Non-fluent readers often read these words with the same stress and pauses as they give content words. We call this word-by-word reading. Alternatively, fluent readers stress the content words and not the function words and shift the vowel pronunciation to the schwa rather than the vowel that is printed. Weber (2006) concludes,

> As young children build up their proficiency in reading, they must draw the connections between printed words that they see on the page with forms in speech that they have hardly noticed that carry weak stress, variable pronunciations, and tenuous but necessary meaning in sentences. [Beginning readers] distort the prosody of English by reading, in the extreme, word by word. They may often lose track of the identity of a particular function word in the context of complex sentences. But as they consolidate their knowledge, they build up their fluency and approach the rhythm of strong and weak syllables of familiar speech. (p. 267)

Weber (in press) also notes the potential problems that direct quotations can create for beginning readers. Use of quotations is common in children's reading materials, and the difficulties they present have been largely overlooked. Consider that when people speak, they almost always say something like, "Mom said, 'It was time to go.' " But in print, authors write this more commonly as, " 'It was time to go,' Mom said." And although "I said," "She said," and "He said" are common in speaking, authors often write "he growled," "snapped Dad," or "whined Billy." Two problems appear here. One is the use of less common words to replace *said* in writing. The other is that the usual sequence in speech for marking a speaker is noun-verb (I said), but in print, that order is almost always reversed to verb-noun (replied Ann).

In other words, writing is rarely talk written down. When people write, they use different conventions from those they commonly use when speaking. Thus, beginning readers need to learn these conventions of texts, and until they do, fluent reading will be unlikely.

Weber (in press) notes other difficulties such as this excerpt from Cynthia Rylant's *Henry and Mudge* series:

> Henry's mother was thinking.
> "I know," she said. "A bunny!
> It's soft and dry and
> doesn't fly."
> "And it doesn't have to be
> walked like a dog," said Henry. (Rylant, 2000)

In this example, the speaker shifts with no clear marker. We don't find out it is Henry who is speaking the last two lines until we get to the end of the last line. Additionally, the marker for Henry's mom's talk is inserted midway through the dialogue.

Although Weber's (2006; in press) articles are a bit technical, they serve to remind educators that developing fluent readers takes much more than producing children who can read words accurately and quickly. In fact to read fluently, children must learn to adjust their pronunciation of function words based on the role that a particular word is playing in a text. They have to learn, for instance, to not pronounce *can* as /can/ but instead as /kin/ in some situations if they want to be heard as reading fluently. When they read printed dialogue they have to learn that the way a speaker is marked in print is different from the way it is done when speaking. The fact that most beginning readers become fluent readers with little attention paid to all of this is almost a miracle, in my view.

☆ Phrasing

There is a similar sort of development in reading words in phrases. Fluent readers don't read word-by-word nor do they read in random 2- or 3-word clusters of words. Fluent readers read in phrases, and when they get the phrasing wrong, listeners can hear it. One supposes that that these beginning readers often can hear it as well.

How is it that most beginning readers figure out which words to read as a phrase? This too is a little researched topic. Nonetheless, it is an important accomplishment, once again fostered by little instructional direction. What researchers do know is that most of the mistakes readers make when reading reflect their knowledge of English syntax. That is, most errors readers make replace a verb with a verb and a noun with a noun and so on (Biemiller, 1970; Weber, 1970). This suggests again that knowledge of spoken English plays a role in fluent reading. And since there are only a few clues in printed English that help with phrasing (commas, periods, and other end punctuation marks), readers must rely on what they know about phrasing while speaking as they begin to read in phrases. Here again the topic can get a bit technical with terms such as *pitch, juncture,* and *stress* all coming into play when reading fluently and in appropriate phrases.

Nonetheless, fluent readers, even young fluent readers, typically read the following sentence in these phrases:

John threw the ball/over the fence.

Fluent readers don't read the sentence like this:

John threw the/ball over/the fence.

Note that in this sentence the only visual marker for any phrasing is the period at the end of the sentence. That period indicates a full stop (or terminal juncture). Nothing indicates which words go together as an appropriate phrase. And if the sentence was a response to the question from an adult (*OK, who threw the ball away?*), the appropriate reading would put stress on *John* as in:

JOHN threw the ball over the fence.

In this case, the phrasing might well be:

JOHN/threw the ball/over the fence.

However, if the adult's question was, *How did the ball get over there?*, the appropriate response might be to put the stress on the word *threw* as in:

John THREW the ball/over the fence.

No matter how one considers it, learning to read in phrases is important and again is typically accomplished with little instructional guidance. And, as with learning about the appropriate pronunciation of function words when reading aloud, the reader must draw largely on what he or she knows about phrasing from speaking English. However, fostering fluent reading in the classroom may not require many changes in the typical early reading lesson. I say this because most beginning readers have always figured out all of this complicated stuff without much help from their teachers. Nonetheless, there are some things classroom teachers might do to assist beginning readers in becoming fluent and several things that may hinder fluency development that they must reconsider.

★ Supporting the Development of Fluent Readers

Although most beginning readers become fluent readers (reading accurately in phrases with expression and comprehension), it might be that teachers could promote more rapid development of fluent reading and in more children if teachers routinely engaged in a few helpful classroom activities.

Teacher Modeling and Rereading

As noted earlier, the role of adults reading aloud to children seems to be a critical contributor to the development of fluent reading. Thus, I suggest that all children will benefit from listening to the teacher read aloud every day. This seems especially important for any children who arrived at school with few read-aloud experiences. Deborah Smith (1979) demonstrated that teacher modeling of fluent reading produced positive changes in the fluency and accuracy of early readers. In this study, Smith simply read aloud the first few pages of a story before having the students read the story themselves.

Along similar lines, Eldredge, Reutzel, and Hollingsworth (1996) compared using round-robin reading of stories to engaging students in the shared book experience (SBE), which included a model of a teacher read-aloud of the story the children would read. The authors reported that on every measure used in this experiment the children who were exposed to the teacher modeling (SBE treatment) significantly outperformed the children exposed to round-robin reading of the same stories. The gains produced by the SBE lessons were quite dramatic, with differences of 20 to 30 percentile ranks on the Iowa Test of Basic Skills as well as substantially better fluency, word analysis, and comprehension measures. Effect sizes of .46 to 1.0 were reported in the SBE treatment comparisons.

This same research team (Reutzel, Eldredge, & Hollingsworth, 1994) also demonstrated the superiority of the SBE with its modeling component to the

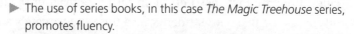

▶ The use of series books, in this case *The Magic Treehouse* series, promotes fluency.

more traditional oral reading lesson design found in many commercial reading series. Again, the lesson with teacher modeling of fluent reading produced significantly greater gains in all areas assessed.

Rasinski and Hoffman (2003) reviewed the research on oral reading as it related to the development of fluency. They noted that oral reading shifted from reading for expression in the early twentieth century to a procedure for checking on word recognition accuracy more recently. Thus, the assessment of fluency through oral reading was largely neglected until recently. However, as fluency has again become one focus of reading adequacy, the authors report on a variety of research studies examining different models of reading lessons for their impact on fluency development.

The shared book experience was described by Rasinski and Hoffman (2003) as one model for a reading lesson that focuses on fluency and expression. In SBE lessons, the teacher reads the text to the class and then discusses it with them. The students read and reread the text with their teacher, with classmates, and on their own. They describe the SBE as one instance of direct fluency instruction.

The oral recitation lesson (ORL) framework is another model that provides direct fluency instruction. In ORL the teacher reads the text to students, discusses the text with students, and then they create a summary together. Next, the students reread the text with the teacher and finally select a story segment to perform orally. This segment is practiced with the teacher and classmates and then performed. The students also select passages from previous lessons to practice and perform. The teacher records student accuracy and fluency on all performed passages and uses this information to select instructional features that may need attention.

Fluency Oriented Reading Instruction (FORI; Stahl & Heubach, 2005) is similar to ORL in that passages from a basal reader are selected for practice over a number of days, usually with a partner alternating pages, and students read these to parents at home. Often students will read and reread a story or basal selection 10 to 15 times in a week.

All of these redesigned oral reading lessons proved more beneficial than traditional round-robin reading on a variety of measures with various types of readers.

In each of these alternatives to the traditional reading lesson, one finds teacher modeling of fluent oral reading as a prominent component. Additionally, student rereading of the passage is another common component. This use of the repeated readings strategy was identified by the National Reading Panel (2000) as consistently supported by the research. But repeated readings as an instructional strategy should be used with moderation because it limits the total number of new words that children will read, and the total number of words children read is an important component of fluency development, as will be explained shortly.

Summary   Summarizing what the research says about supporting the development of fluency in primary-grade reading lessons includes noting the important role that teacher modeling of fluent reading plays. Such modeling can be done in a variety of ways:

- Reading aloud from children's literature
- Reading aloud and tracking print with big books
- Rereading language experience charts that were developed with the children
- Reading aloud in the SBE, ORL, or FORI lesson models
- Reading aloud the weekly story from the core reading program as children follow along

Similarly, having children reread stories or passages is another well-supported lesson component for fostering fluency. This rereading can be accomplished in a number of ways also (more details on some of these methods will be presented in Chapter 5):

- Rereading after the teacher has read the story aloud
- Rereading as a choral reading activity with some or all classmates and the teacher
- Rereading as a partner reading activity
- Rereading as independent seatwork activity
- Rereading and practicing some segment of a story for presentation to class

Both teacher modeling and some rereading activity foster fluency in young readers. Unfortunately, though, it isn't quite that easy. While ensuring these two lesson components are regular features of classroom instruction, there are other critical components that must be considered as well.

Appropriate Texts

In order to read fluently, all readers need texts that they can read with a high degree of accuracy and automaticity. When readers are provided with texts that are too difficult, fluent reading is impossible.

Think about your own reading fluency. Everyone encounters too-difficult texts some of the time. Generally, adults usually don't bother finishing reading such texts. Consider that article from a cognitive psychology journal one of your professors distributed as an assignment. Here is what usually happens: You read the introductory section and maybe even the literature review. But when you get to the sections on research methods, statistical analyses, and the results as displayed in various quantitative tables, you decide to skim or skip and go right to the summary, discussion, and conclusions sections. Even these sections may seem problematic if your oral reading fluency was measured.

Now think about your response to an article in a professional journal from a field far different from education—perhaps something from a nanotechnology journal or an ophthamological journal. You get the point.

Having a large word meaning vocabulary makes fluent reading easier. If you suspect that many students in your classroom have limited meaning vocabularies, you may want to read Patricia Cunningham's *What Really Matters in Vocabulary* (Allyn & Bacon, 2009), one of the other titles in this series. This practical book provides explicit lesson guidelines for fostering the acquisition of word meanings during guided reading, teacher read-alouds, and other common classroom activities.

Even skilled readers encounter texts that they cannot read aloud with accuracy and expression.

When beginning or struggling readers are provided with a steady diet of books that are too difficult for them to read, they stumble through the text, reading with low accuracy and often word-by-word. Indeed, they exhibit the same oral reading behaviors that skilled readers do when given too-difficult texts. And when beginning or struggling readers are provided with a steady diet of too-difficult texts, they may begin to habituate that word-by-word reading style. Then, even when they have a text they can read accurately, they read word-by-word because that is how they've been trained to read.

The point is that to foster fluency development, readers need a steady diet of high-success texts to read (Allington, 2006b). Once again, although there is too little research on just how accurately texts must be read to foster fluency development, experts do know some things that are important about text difficulty.

Accuracy

The research and professional literature is replete with recommended accuracy levels. The most common seems to be reading with at least 95 percent accuracy. In other words, no more than 1 misread word in every 20 words read. That accuracy percentage seems justified if the reader is involved with some sort of guided reading activity. In such cases the teacher is available to support the reading and provide guidance when needed. This support might take the form of providing a shared reading of the story before the reader reads it aloud. It might also involve introducing some key new words before the story is read aloud.

Generally speaking, however, I think the 95 percent accuracy level is too liberal if the reader is attempting to read independently. Here, a 98 or 99 percent accuracy seems more appropriate. That is one or two wrong words out of 100 words read.

Consider that by the middle of first grade, the books that a typically developing reader would be reading contain around 150 to 300 running words (books like those featuring Biscuit, the puppy, in the *My First I Can Read* series published by Harper Trophy). At a 98 percent accuracy level, a reader would mispronounce or omit 3 to 6 words. By the end of first grade, typically developing readers are reading books like those found in the *Junie B. Jones* series, where there are 100 to 150 words *per page*. In these books, then, a 98 percent accuracy rate would mean there would be 2 or 3 words on every page the reader would be unable to read accurately.

When was the last time you read a text where there were 2 or 3 words on every page you could not pronounce? Keep in mind that there are 200 to 300 words on every page in most adult books, so a 98 percent accuracy rate would mean that there were 4 to 6 words on *every page* you could not pronounce.

How Accuracy Effects Fluency Development

A high level of accuracy when reading is an essential aspect of fostering fluency. Perhaps the most critical skill in fluent reading is the ability to recognize a great many words "at a glance." This is what has been called *automaticity*. Automatic word recognition is when you recognize the word with little conscious effort (thus, "at-a-glance" recognition).

Developing an at-a-glance store of words requires readers to encounter the word repeatedly and with each encounter read it accurately. It doesn't seem to matter whether the word is read successfully aloud or silently, so long as it is accurate reading (deJong & Share, 2007).

While much attention has been paid recently to the importance of developing the decoding skills in the primary grades, less attention has been paid to the development of at-a-glance words. Marilyn Adams (1990) discussed the critical nature of what she dubbed the "orthographic processor." This is the system that allows words to be recognized at a glance. It is this system that allows fluent reading to develop and thrive.

The basic theory that underlies the notion of at-a-glance word recognition indicates that after multiple (10 to 25) successful pronunciations of a word, that word is now recognized as a whole. At this point, there is no longer any need to sound the word out. At a glance, words are then recognized very quickly and require the use of little cognitive attention. These are the words researchers find that readers can identify within milliseconds after they are flashed on a screen. How many words can be recognized at a glance is critical to fluent reading.

High levels of accuracy when reading are necessary to develop at-a-glance word recognition because it takes repeated *accurate* readings of a word to turn it into an at-a-glance word. Every time a word is misread there is the strong possibility for lingering confusion over just how that pattern of letters is pronounced. In many respects this need for high accuracy is why developing decoding skills is one important aspect of becoming a successful reader.

Everyone who has ever taught primary-grade reading has observed this phenomenon. On a first exposure to a word in a story, say the word *farm*, the child laboriously sounds the word out. However, by the end of the story, after reading the word *farm* correctly 7 times, the reader no longer sounds the word out but simply pronounces it. The next day, in a new story, if the word *farm* appears it is still recognized quickly with no sounding out observed.

Texts and Fluency

For words to develop as at-a-glance words, the reader needs to repeatedly read them successfully. One reason, I believe, for the success of the repeated readings strategy is that it provides just these opportunities. Likewise, when the teacher models reading the text aloud to students before they read, it seems more likely that children will successfully identify those words they have not seen before. But for developing fluency, the core reading programs in classrooms today have several disadvantages, especially when teachers follow the standard guided reading lesson they provide. This is because today's core reading program materials feature far more rare words (twice as many as were found in the pre-1990 readers) and far more words that appear only once in a story (Hiebert & Fisher, 2005). When you couple these two factors with a standard lesson design that does not feature repeated reading of the text and provides no teacher modeling, you have a plan for inhibiting the development of reading fluency.

Hiebert and Fisher (2005) noted that controlled vocabulary texts were used in roughly three of four fluency studies reviewed by the NRP. But today's (post-1990) core basal reading programs feature far less control of vocabulary and include many more rare words that appear only a single time. In the four fluency studies reviewed by NRP that used post-1990 texts, only one reported a positive fluency outcome and that was not statistically significant. These researchers conclude that the NRP recommendations on repeated readings as a method for building fluency is supported only if controlled texts, not today's reading series, are used.

Too often educators assume that grade-level core reading texts consistently provide appropriately difficult texts for students to read. However, Hiebert (2002) reports that one third-grade basal included a 6.0 readability (810 lexile) selection as well as a 2.0 readability (430 lexile). In this core reader, books or excerpts that were identified as appropriate ranged from *The Night Crossing* (Ackerman, 1994, Knopf) with a readability of 6.5 (lexile 960), *Leah's Pony* (Friedrich, 1996, Boyds Mills) at 2.0 readability (lexile 560), and *Beezus and Ramona* (Cleary, 1955, Avon) with a 5.3 readability (lexile 780). The texts students were expected to read in the pool of third-grade core reading programs ranged across five to seven grade levels on readability levels, and the lexile ratings ranged from grade 2 to grade 6 and above. Similar ranges were reported by McGill-Franzen and colleagues (2006) in their analysis of third-grade core reading programs.

Hiebert and Fisher (2005) have also reported that today's core basals have twice as many rare/infrequent words (e.g., *lad, moan, adamant, hasten, enthusiastic*) as the older core readers that featured more controlled texts. These rare words often appear only a single time in a story and thus provide few opportunities for repeated successful encounters needed to foster recognition as well as the acquisition of that word's meaning. Today many state and school district policies stress use of a core basal program in the classroom and also emphasize the importance of fluency development. But today's basals do not provide the sort of controlled vocabulary texts that previous research indicated were effective in developing fluency in repeated reading lessons.

So what to do? One might consider locating some of the older reading materials for fluency lessons. Alternatively, adding both teacher modeling and repeated readings of some of the stories being read should help minimize the problem found in the core reading materials of today.

One might simply add the fluency development lesson to the regular reading instruction lesson (Rasinski & Hoffman, 2003). This is a 15-minute daily add-on where students read and reread a passage of appropriate difficulty, often a poem. The initial reading is by the teacher, followed by several group choral readings of the same passage with the teacher. Then students practice rereading the text three times each with a classmate. The passage can then be performed for the class.

☆ Summary

Fostering fluency development is one important aspect of reading lessons, but remember that most children acquire fluent reading abilities with little teacher attention to the topic. This chapter has noted that fluency development is more complicated than it may seem, but be wary of overemphasizing fluency. A focus on fluency may be most appropriate with children who struggle with its development. That is the topic of the next chapter.

chapter 3

Why Do Some Readers Struggle with Fluency?

As I noted earlier, most beginning readers develop into fluent readers with little instructional attention to fluency, but some beginning readers never seem to move beyond word-by-word reading. They struggle, often for years, even after effective decoding instruction has enabled them to read reasonably accurately (Torgeson & Hudson, 2006).

This longstanding finding was indicated by Lyon and Moats (1997) in their decade-old review of intervention research: "It is critical to recognize that in all NICHD intervention studies to date, improvements in decoding and word reading accuracy have been far easier to obtain than improvement in reading fluency and automaticity" (p. 583).

So why is it that some students continue to struggle with fluency? In this chapter I set out an argument that suggests that most fluency problems are instructionally induced and instructionally maintained. I have made this argument earlier (Allington, 2006b; 2007a) and believe the research supports this view. However, I must also note that no experimental studies, the federal "gold standard" for evidence, are available to support my view.

There is a good reason that such studies do not exist. In order to "prove" that instructional factors foster dysfluent reading, one would have to design a study to intentionally create dysfluent readers. Although I have a good idea of just how to design that study, ethically I cannot do so. As a practical manner, even if I could get over my ethical concerns, federal regulations on research conducted with minors requires that I get the informed consent from parents or guardians (as well as the consent of a school district) to demonstrate that I can design lessons that will hinder fluency development. I would hope that I am correct in assuming that no parent (or school district) would allow me to implement an instructional design that would purposely hinder the development of fluent readers.

But if I were to design a program that would foster dysfluent reading, I would create lessons where readers were:

- Given a steady diet of too-difficult texts, texts they cannot read accurately

- Offered daily lessons that provide little high-success reading opportunity so that very little actual reading is completed

- Lessons where teachers, or others, frequently, consistently, and immediately interrupt readers when they misread a word

Unfortunately, this lesson design reflects many of the characteristics of the actual lessons that many struggling readers receive. In other words, I will suggest that "natural experiments," observations of variations in classroom instruction, already provide the needed research evidence to support my argument about why many beginning readers never develop into fluent readers and why the most common lesson design of intervention programs produces little growth in fluency. In the remainder of this chapter I will review the available research that supports my argument and close with recommendations for the redesign of reading lessons for struggling readers.

☆ Too-Difficult Texts

Every reader, even a rather proficient reader, has fluency problems when given texts to read that are hard for them. The texts may be hard because they contain many rare, long, or hard-to-pronounce words. The texts may be difficult because the topic is wholly unfamiliar to the reader. When teachers routinely provide texts that are too hard, there is little opportunity for students to develop fluent reading skills.

Unfortunately, a long line of classroom observational research indicates that too-difficult texts are precisely what struggling readers are usually asked to read (Allington, 1983a; Gambrell, Wilson, & Gantt, 1981; Hiebert, 1983; Jorgenson, 1977; O'Connor et al., 2002; Vaughn et al., 2003). This occurs when a grade-level, one-size-fits-all core curriculum is put in place and all students are provided reading instruction in that curriculum material. In such situations the curriculum material may be of a level of difficulty that makes it appropriate for use with the normally achieving readers. But the reading material will be too challenging for those readers whose achievement has lagged behind.

For instance, in a third-grade classroom there may be five or more students whose reading development is closer to that of normally developing second-grade students than normally developing third-graders. The typical third-grade core reading program is supposed to be comprised primarily of stories of a level of difficulty appropriate for third-grade readers. (I noted the research earlier that demonstrates that this assumption has been disproven and that many of the texts will be hard even for normally developing readers.) That third-grade core reading program material will pose substantial difficulties for the struggling readers in the third-grade classroom. Teachers will also find that current core basal reading programs offer little instructional advice to teachers on how the lessons might be adapted for the struggling readers (McGill-Franzen et al., 2006).

Alternatively, consider the students in sixth grade whose reading development is similar to that of typical third-grade students. These are just the sorts of students that O'Connor and colleagues (2002) studied in their experimental intervention. The study compared three approaches to educating struggling readers. In the first, students were tutored using grade-level materials from their classrooms. The second group of struggling readers were tutored in materials matched to their reading level (e.g., third-grade materials). The control group was not provided any tutoring. Both tutored groups had larger gains in reading than the control group. But the group of students tutored in materials at their reading level made significantly greater fluency gains than did the group tutored in classroom grade-level materials. The researchers concluded that the reading-level tutoring produced the largest gains in fluency, word recognition, and comprehension for lowest-achieving students, those least likely to be able to read grade-level materials even with tutorial support. It seems clear from this study that struggling readers are not likely to improve their fluency when given grade-level materials.

However, if one examines the texts that typical struggling sixth-grade readers have in their desks (or lockers, backpacks, etc.), one typically finds a bunch of texts of sixth-grade difficulty or higher (Allington, 2007b). There may be a sixth-grade reading or literature anthology as well as sixth-grade science, social studies, and health textbooks (all of which are likely to have difficulty levels above the sixth-grade level). So just what are these struggling sixth-graders supposed to read? If there is a classroom library collection, it is likely that almost all of the books in that collection are at the fifth- or sixth-grade level or higher. This means there would also be no classroom library books that the struggling sixth-grade readers can read. In fact, it is this dominant supply of grade-level reading materials that is the main reason struggling readers don't read very much. And because they don't read much, they remain struggling readers.

If struggling readers cannot read grade-level texts fluently or be taught to read fluently with those texts, what is a teacher to do? The research clearly indicates that the solution is to locate appropriately difficult texts for the reading lessons (and for science, social studies, and health classes).

What is an appropriate level of difficulty for a struggling reader and what is a too-hard text? If fostering fluency is the goal, then I suggest that any text that cannot be read with 99 percent accuracy is probably too difficult. In such a text a reader would mispronounce or purposely skip over one word in every 100 running words of text. That would be roughly 1 word every second or third page in a beginning book such as *Frog and Toad* by Arnold Lobel. But in other elementary-grade texts, readers would be missing 1 or more words on every page (see Table 3.1).

The percentages in the table were selected because different authors have recommended these various levels of accuracy as appropriate for fluency work and for independent reading. But quite honestly, I am not sure that 99 percent accuracy is high enough for fluency practice or for independent reading, at least with older elementary readers. Can you imagine reading a text where you found 3 words on every page you couldn't read, as would be the case of reading with 99 percent accuracy in one of the Harry Potter books? That 99 percent accuracy level would result in over 50 words that you wouldn't be able to read in the first chapter of the first Harry Potter book!

Realistically speaking, most of those 50+ words that would be read inaccurately would be words important to the story—words such as *mysterious, opinion, cloaks, concentrate, imagination, horribly, quiver, irritably, impatiently, astonishing, furiously, tidy, visible, sensible, piercing, rummaging, unblinkingly, contrary, gazed, shuddered,* and *chortled.* These 21 words come from the opening

▶ Table 3.1 **Number of errors per page at different accuracy rates in elementary texts**

	95%	98%	99%
Junie B. Jones (Park) series	5.0	2.0	1.0
Time Warp Trio (Scieszka) series	7.5	3.0	1.5
Wind in the Willows (Grahame)	11.0	4.0	2.0
Harry Potter (Rowling) series	16.0	6.0	3.0

Note: These estimates may vary a little depending on the edition of the book.

chapter of the first Harry Potter book. Now imagine that there are 30 more words you cannot read. If a reader misread or skipped over 50 such words in that first chapter, comprehension would be nil, so as to make fluent reading impossible.

There are two reasons that high levels of accuracy are essential for fostering fluency. First, and perhaps most obviously, it is impossible to read in phrases with expression if the individual has to frequently stop and figure out words (or at least try to). In such cases, much cognitive capacity is allocated to decoding/word recognition, and so little is left to allocate to parsing the sentence into appropriate phrase units and for the assignment of intonation and so on.

The second reason high levels of accuracy are important is related to the first but is basically a different issue. As noted earlier, readers become fluent as they develop larger and larger numbers of words that can be recognized at a glance. But to increase this store of at-a-glance words, readers need to consistently and repeatedly read a word correctly. The development of this essential component of fluent and skilled reading then requires accurate reading—a *lot* of accurate reading. Thus, the importance of the volume of reading that readers do is discussed in the next section.

★ Reading Volume and Fluency Development

I have argued that a critical factor in designing interventions for struggling readers is ensuring that these students read at least as much as the achieving readers at their grade level (Allington, 2006b). Virtually every study of reading volume indicates that struggling readers engage in far less reading than do achieving readers. Both Stanovich and West (1989) and Share and Stanovich (1995) point out that it is extensive engagement in high-accuracy reading that allows readers to consolidate the various skills and components of proficient reading. When struggling readers are provided with a limited amount of such practice, they simply do not develop the skills and components that are essential for proficient, autonomous reading.

Guthrie (2004) has noted the substantial differences in the volume of reading that struggling and achieving readers do. He uses the available research to estimate that students whose reading skills are below the 25th percentile read about 30 minutes daily. At the 50th percentile, readers read about 120 minutes a day, and those at the 75th percentile read about 210 minutes daily. After 60 to 90 minutes of daily in-school reading, the remaining time is largely spent engaged in voluntary reading outside of school. By third grade, for instance, these routine differences in reading volume mean that the better readers have read *millions* more words than the struggling readers. That means that the better readers have successfully read the 3,000 most frequent words in English so many times that these words are almost surely words they recognize at a glance.

Having this large number of words recognized with little cognitive effort means that these readers can now focus on fluency, comprehension, and self-regulation while reading. But the struggling readers face a huge obstacle in ever becoming fluent. Torgeson and Hudson (2006) explain:

> This difficulty in recovering the "lost ground" in the development of sight-word vocabulary that results from several years of minimal and inaccurate reading is the simplest current explanation for the enduring reading fluency problems of students even after they become more accurate readers through strong reading [*decoding emphasis*] interventions. (pp. 152–153)

Thus, the research available shows that developing decoding skills, a common intervention concern, is simply not sufficient to foster fluent reading. Rather, the research indicates that successful interventions must focus on substantial increases in the volume of high-accuracy reading that struggling readers do if fluency problems are to be overcome.

One reason that the research on repeated reading interventions has demonstrated the positive outcomes that the NRP emphasized is that this intervention design reliably increases the volume of reading done by struggling readers. Additionally, repeatedly reading passages produces high-accuracy reading along with multiple successful encounters with the most common English words. In other words, the typical repeated reading intervention addresses both problems of too hard texts and too little reading activity.

There have been two major recent reviews of the research on the repeated readings strategy (Kuhn & Stahl, 2003; National Reading Panel, 2000). Both point to the largely consistent evidence that the technique of repeated readings improves the reading fluency of struggling readers. Less clear is whether it improves other reading proficiencies. But much of the repeated readings research is fundamentally flawed, according to Kuhn and Stahl (2003). This is because most studies of repeated readings did not have the control groups engaged in reading while the treatment groups engaged in repeated readings of texts. Thus, it may simply be that the positive effects of repeated readings derive mostly from increasing the volume of reading that the treatment students did. There have been a few studies where the control groups read independently for the same amount of time that the treatment students spent completing their repeated readings activities. In those few studies that included equal amounts of independent reading, the independent reading and repeated readings interventions produced similar positive effects on both fluency and accuracy (cf. Homan, Klesius, & Hite, 1993; Rashotte & Torgeson, 1985). In other words, simply increasing the volume of reading produced the same positive effects on reading fluency and word recognition as the repeated readings intervention strategy.

Noting this finding, Kuhn (2005a, 2005b) has experimentally compared extensive independent reading with repeated reading interventions. Kuhn assessed reading fluency gains as well as gains on other reading proficiencies. She reported that increasing the volume of independent reading produced comprehension gains that the repeated readings technique did not. Kuhn commented on the fact that the traditional repeated readings strategy had no comprehension focus and suggested that perhaps the focus on fluency, rate, and accuracy may have biased the students in the repeated reading interventions such that reading aloud fast and fluently became the goal, and understanding what was read became relatively unimportant.

Recently Kuhn and colleagues (2007) compared a repeated readings intervention with what they called a wide reading intervention in a large-scale study. The basic difference in these two lesson models was how much unique text students read. Both groups did some repeated readings of texts but the wide reading groups did fewer repeated readings and, instead, read lots of other texts. The repeated readings groups simply read and reread the same small number of texts. Both groups, however, were engaged in reading for equivalent amounts of time each day. The authors concluded, "The current study confirms that, not only did the Wide Reading approach do as well as the FORI [repeated readings] approach, it was actually more effective for the participating students in two areas: first, improvements were seen sooner and, second, improvements were seen in connected text reading" (p. 27).

The available research on reading volume should make educators consider whether the major source of the problem of dysfluent readers is primarily one of limited opportunities for high-accuracy reading practice (Allington, 1984; 2006b; Guthrie, 2004). If struggling readers routinely do much less reading (as every study of this topic indicates) and especially if they have substantially fewer opportunities to engage in high-accuracy reading (as studies also indicate), then perhaps researchers have located the primary reason these struggling readers have failed to develop into fluent and engaged readers. If so, then teachers don't have to try to explain this lack of fluency by relying on conceptually muddy ideas such as learning disabilities, neurological damage, and attention deficits as the source of the fluency problem. Instead of creating pseudo-scientific labels for struggling readers, teachers can create better instructional environments and observe as fluency problems largely vanish.

If teachers give some students a steady diet of texts that are too difficult and thus offer them limited opportunities to practice high-accuracy reading, then teachers should expect that many of their students will experience difficulties in becoming fluent and engaged readers. Additionally, too-hard texts and lots of oral reading during reading lessons create a third instructional factor that works against developing fluent engaged readers.

☆ Interruptive Reading and Fluency Development (Or the Lack of It)

Researchers have well documented that struggling readers are more likely to be asked to read aloud in the classroom than are the achieving readers (Allington, 1983b; Chinn et al., 1993; Hiebert, 1983). Often this reading aloud occurs during a directed reading lesson when each child reads aloud a bit, in turn. It is in such lessons that teachers are far more likely to interrupt the lower-achieving readers than the higher-achieving readers. Teachers are also more likely to interrupt poor readers more quickly, usually immediately following the incorrect pronunciation of a word. They are also most likely to ask the reader to "sound the word out" (Allington, 1980; Chinn et al., 1993; Hoffman et al., 1984). Teachers also allow other readers to interrupt struggling readers but discourage such interruptions when the better readers read aloud (Eder & Felmlee, 1984). These studies provide sound evidence that teachers interact differently with their achieving and struggling readers.

It is not clear why teachers respond so differently when good and poor readers read aloud. I think that teachers are typically attempting to help, to support, their struggling readers. It may be that because the struggling readers are too often reading from too-hard texts, the teacher realizes that they may not have the skills to figure out the word they misread. In other words, the common use of too-difficult texts with struggling readers creates a situation that calls out for teacher interventions. Alternatively, it may be that teachers hold general beliefs about the inability of struggling readers to solve problems independently and so they try to prompt or cue the readers to figure out the misread word. Or, perhaps because the text is so difficult the struggling readers are misreading so many more words that the teacher feels it necessary to intervene.

Nonetheless, the frequent and immediate interruptions have the potential, in and of themselves, to create not just dysfluent readers but also passive, dependent readers (Johnston & Winograd, 1985). Dependent readers rely on someone else to solve their problems, or what is called "learned helplessness" (Dweck, 1986). These readers typically have very limited ability to monitor their own reading and use fix-up strategies when they encounter difficulty.

Consider that struggling readers often encounter reading lessons where they will:

- Be asked to read aloud
- Be reading too-hard texts
- Be interrupted when they misread a word
- Be interrupted immediately after misreading
- Be asked to sound the word out

Contrast this scenario with what research reveals achieving readers typically encounter in their reading lesson. These students will:

- Be reading material of an appropriate level of difficulty
- Be asked to read silently
- Be expected to self-monitor and self-correct
- Have attention focused on understanding
- Be interrupted only after a wait period or at the end of a sentence
- Be asked to reread or to self-monitor their reading when interrupted

Given the striking differences that researchers have documented in the most common lesson design, is it any wonder that struggling readers do not read the same way that achieving readers do?

For me, the central and most critical problem is the immediate interruption when readers misread. I think this may be one of those holdovers from the era of behaviorist psychology, an era when it was thought that not correcting immediately would cause mislearning. Although there is some truth to that view, there is another unfortunate result of interrupting immediately. That result is that interrupting so quickly does not allow the reader to engage in self-monitoring of the reading. It is the case that for most English sentences, a misread word will become obviously wrong only when the reader continues reading to the end of the sentence.

Consider the reader who misreads *struck* as *stuck* in this sentence:

John stuck out on a curve ball.

Reading to the end of the sentence makes it obvious that a misreading has occurred (assuming the reader is monitoring his or her reading and knows something of the vocabulary of baseball). But if the teacher interrupts as soon as the misreading occurs (immediately after *stuck* is uttered), it is impossible for the child to recognize that the combination of words do not make any sense because "*John stuck . . .*" is a legal construction. In such a case the teacher cannot prompt the reader to self-monitor for meaning. This largely explains why a teacher typically then directs the reader's attention to the word (*sound it out*) rather than to monitoring meaning.

Here is another example of the same sort where I note the critical implications of such "help."

> Ultimately, the reader fully accepts the external monitoring and no longer self-monitors his reading activity. Thus, we can observe these pupils read the sentence A below as sentence B.
>
> A. John lives in a big white house.
> B. John lives in a big white HORSE.
>
> This sort of substitution provides powerful evidence that the interruptive external monitoring has largely eliminated self-monitoring while reading. If you were to ask this reader, "What color HORSE do you live in?", he would invariably ask, "Do you mean HOUSE?" This pupil will never speak a sentence that confuses *house/horse* but with sufficient amounts of too hard reading along with interruptive monitoring, we can eliminate from his reading repertoire this language self-monitoring that he uses in literally every other language context. (Allington, 2007a, p. 3)

Teachers who interrupt immediately and when interruptions come frequently because the text is too hard create passive readers who rely more on the teacher to monitor their reading than on self-monitoring. But self-monitoring, independently and spontaneously correcting misread words, is a critical proficiency if one hopes to develop fluent and engaged readers (Clay, 1969; Walczyk & Griffith-Ross, 2007). Rasinski and Hoffman (2003) noted that a single, but widely cited, study of pupils with disabilities has been used to support immediate interruption after an oral reading error. That study has not been replicated, however, and the findings are at odds with other studies (e.g., Hoffman et al., 1984) that demonstrated a detrimental effect for immediate feedback compared to other options such as focusing on self-monitoring.

Fluency development is disrupted when pupils are (1) routinely given too-hard texts and (2) frequently interrupted while they read. In far too many lessons struggling readers receive one or both of these conditions. When struggling readers read a text that is too difficult, they make many errors. Then the teacher feels compelled to interrupt and attempt to get the struggling reader to produce an accurate reading of the text. Over time, the struggling reader begins to read aloud more tentatively and waits for the teacher to confirm or reject the words as he or she reads them aloud. Eventually the reader and the teacher develop a reciprocal response pattern where the reader hesitates awaiting a confirmation from the teacher that the reading is correct, the teacher supplies a confirmation (e.g., "right," "uh-huh," "good job"), then the struggling reader continues on to the next word and engages in the same verbal dance with the teacher (Allington, 1980; McGill-Franzen & McDermott, 1978). As the reader becomes ever more dependent on the teacher to confirm or reject his or her responses, the reader hesitates more frequently and so the interruptions/confirmations also increase. Ultimately, the struggling reader becomes increasingly passive regarding self-monitoring, and his or her reading is now routinely word-by-word.

Modifying the reading lessons provided to the struggling readers so that there are few immediate interruptions while also focusing on improving their self-monitoring will be easier if teachers ensure that struggling readers have texts they can read accurately. Altering the struggling readers' lessons in this way may also increase the volume of reading.

Some children fail to develop adequate fluency for another reason: They have had limited reading practice, particularly practice in high-success texts. High-success reading experiences are characterized by accurate, fluent reading with good understanding of the text that was read. It is this sort of reading that too often seems in short supply in the reading experiences of struggling readers.

★ Some Concerns about the Repeated Readings Technique

The NRP (2000) reviewed the experimental research on interventions that fostered fluency development. The panel concluded that the evidence supported the technique of repeated readings as an evidence-based intervention.

In general, I agree. However, I am worried about the sudden emergence of several commercial intervention programs that entail the long-term use of the repeated readings technique as a general solution for lower-achieving readers.

I visit schools where struggling readers are placed in such intervention programs for a full year or even more! Both the available research and my clinical experience indicate that fostering fluency should typically take only a few weeks, certainly not years. Almost all of the fluency intervention studies the NRP reviewed were 5- to 10-week efforts, and none involved implementing the repeated readings technique over a period of years. Not only is the extended use of repeated readings as a primary intervention strategy unsupported by the research but it may also undermine the acceleration of both fluency and general reading development.

I have taken this stance because the research available suggests that an exclusive use of repeated readings seems to limit the development of comprehension and impinges on vocabulary growth (Kuhn, 2005a). The best advice to be drawn from the research, I believe, is that repeated readings should be viewed primarily as an initial and short-term intervention strategy. An initial intensive dose of repeated readings may be called for if struggling readers persistently read word-by-word. In such cases, the repeated readings technique seems to be a well-researched way to help readers break out of that style of reading and begin to read in phrases with expression.

The repeated readings of the same text limits the number of unique texts and the number of new words the reader encounters. And because the text will be read over and over again, there is little reason to focus on understanding what is being read, at least on the first reading. In addition, in the Kuhn and colleagues' (2007) study, reducing the time spent engaged in repeated readings and expanding the time struggling readers spent reading independently produced fluency gains more quickly and improved accuracy when reading connected text compared to extended use of the repeated readings technique. As with most issues in reading instruction, the use of the repeated readings technique must be guided by the needs of students. It is a useful, but limited, instructional strategy.

★ Summary

Most students become fluent readers without much instructional guidance or support. I think the evidence is clear that teachers can design reading lessons so that virtually all beginning readers acquire the ability to read in phrases with expression and to self-monitor while they read. There are many common features of the reading lessons currently provided to both beginning and struggling readers that must be changed if all readers are to become fluent readers.

The most important change is to ensure that texts of an appropriate level of difficulty are being used in every reading lesson. When some readers are provided continuing lessons with texts that are too hard, fluent reading should not be an expected outcome. And when too-hard texts are used, readers get discouraged with reading and typically begin to avoid it whenever possible. This leads to struggling readers engaging in a minimal amount of reading, further undermining the likelihood they will become fluent and engaged readers. Too-hard texts seem to encourage interruptions by teachers, which then weakens the development of self-monitoring and slows reading to a crawl, which then means struggling readers read fewer words in every lesson than do their achieving peers. This vicious cycle of too-difficult texts, interruptive reading experiences, and limited reading leads predictably to persisting and persistent reading difficulties. Over the course of a few years, then, school systems produce struggling readers who face enormous obstacles to developing fluent reading abilities or high levels of reading proficiency.

Developing fluent readers will be easier if the problematic features of current reading lessons are changed. To become fluent readers, students need to develop:

- Appropriate decoding skills and strategies
- A large vocabulary of words whose meanings they know
- A store of words they can recognize at a glance
- The ability to self-monitor while they read
- The appropriate comprehension strategies to use while they read
- The motivation to read purposely and voluntarily

Fluency is not something that can be developed apart from these other critical aspects of proficient reading. Fluency development should always be on teachers' minds as they plan reading lessons, but that doesn't mean that every lesson is focused on fluency development. Nonetheless, more readers will become fluent readers if teachers place developing fluency on their instructional agenda and monitor its development regularly.

You can view a presentation on fluency given by Dr. Allington by visiting www.learner.org/channel/workshops/teachreading35/session2/index.html.

chapter 4

How Should Fluency Be Assessed?

Since fluency is one critical aspect of proficient reading, it is important that schools have procedures in place to track fluency development. Fluency assessment, particularly the monitoring of development in beginning readers, allows instruction to be modified when fluency difficulties first appear.

Far too many readers in the upper grades struggle with fluency simply because little attention was paid to their fluency problems in the early grades. Too many older readers struggle with fluency and with reading generally because early reading instruction involved too many of the features discussed in Chapter 3. As illustrated so powerfully by Torgeson and Hudson (2006) in their review of prevention and intervention studies, early attention to fluency difficulties produces far more positive outcomes than do interventions that begin after fluency problems have been around for a while.

When readers fail to develop fluent reading abilities early on, they struggle with developing other reading skills and abilities year after year. By the time they complete third grade, their achieving peers have read millions more words, and the word reading deficit undermines all efforts to develop normal reading abilities. Therefore, it is important to monitor fluency early and to continue to monitor the fluency of any reader who is exhibiting fluency difficulties. It is also important to monitor the volume of reading that struggling readers do. The amount of teacher-directed reading may need to be increased for these students, especially if they are either unable or unwilling to read independently.

At this point I must note, however, that assessing and monitoring fluency will not solve fluency difficulties. Once fluency assessments have identified the readers having difficulty, appropriate instructional interventions are essential if fluency problems are to be overcome. This may involve altering the nature of classroom reading lessons, providing powerful reading interventions including special fluency instruction, or both. But, as I noted earlier, far too many fluency difficulties arise as a result of the particular characteristics of many classroom reading lessons. If monitoring the development of fluency in primary-grade classrooms leads to appropriate changes in classroom reading lessons, then fewer students will struggle with fluency and with learning to read.

☆ Fluency: The Great Debate

Fluency has been hijacked (Mathson, Solic, & Allington, 2006). In many schools across the nation, reading speed and accuracy is being regularly assessed but fluency development is not. As noted in Chapter 1, fluency is the ability to read in phrases with expression and comprehension. This was the meaning as developed in automaticity theory (LaBerge & Samuels, 1974), the theoretical foundation for the importance of fluency in reading development. Nonetheless, the most popular assessment tool that schools use to evaluate and monitor fluency development is the *Dynamic Indicators of Basic Early Literacy Skills* (DIBELS; Good & Kaminski, 2002).

Why DIBELS Is Not a Fluency Assessment

The DIBELS assessments (there are several subtests) do assess rate and accuracy of student responses on measures of various subskills. Each of those DIBELS subtests incorporates the word *fluency* in the title—for instance, "Letter Naming Fluency" and "Non-Word Reading Fluency." In all cases, however, the fluency tag is simply not valid (Samuels, 2006). Speed of response is something different from fluency. Accuracy of response is something different from fluency. Certainly the DIBELS tests measure something, but it is not fluency that is being measured. Thus, the DIBELS assessment cannot be considered a reliable and valid assessment of fluency as required under the No Child Left Behind Act. (I will note that there are other similar systems, though less popular, that have most of the same limitations—the AIMSweb assessments, for instance.)

As NRP member Samuels (2007) argues: "One criticism I have of the DIBELS tests is that, despite their labels, they are not valid tests of the construct of fluency as it is widely understood and defined. They only assess accuracy and speed. . . . By attaching the term *fluency* to their tests, they create the false assumption that that is what their tests measure." Samuels is only one of the researchers who have criticized DIBELS for various inadequacies.

Michael Pressley, the former editor of the *Journal of Educational Psychology*, the premier experimental research journal, and his colleagues (Pressley, Hilden, & Shankland, 2005) conducted a multifaceted study of the adequacy of the DIBELS Oral Reading Fluency and Retelling Fluency subtests. They concluded their research report with the following: "Based on available data, the fairest conclusion is that DIBELS mis-predicts reading performance on other assessments much of the time, and at best is a measure of who reads quickly without regard to whether the reader comprehends what is read" (p. 1). The authors noted that one potential danger of the DIBELS was that readers who can read accurately can meet DIBELS rate, accuracy, and comprehension benchmarks for progress even though they may not comprehend much of what they have read. That is because the DIBELS retelling test did not reliably estimate understanding of the material that had been read. Students could obtain a high DIBELS retelling score without recalling much of the information in the passages they had read. And although the DIBELS oral reading scores did correlate with standardized reading achievement test scores, the correlation was weak to modest. In other words, reading fast and accurately did not predict reading proficiency as typically assessed with any high level of accuracy. Markel and Deno (1997) and Altwerger, Jordan, and Shelton (2008) report similar problems with using rate and accuracy assessments to predict reading comprehension.

Likewise, the research of Schilling, Carlisle, Scott, and Zeng (2007) indicated that although DIBELS benchmark scores were reasonably accurate (75%) in identifying readers below the 25th percentile, over one-third of the students who met or exceeded the DIBELS oral reading fluency benchmarks in second and third grade failed to achieve normal reading levels on the state reading assessments. These students had been denied added instructional support based on the "adequacy" of their DIBELS performances. The DIBELS assessments indicated they were achieving readers, but the reading achievement of these students, their comprehension especially, was actually lagging behind. Such unreliable assessments prove extremely costly in states and school districts where failing to achieve the state reading standard leads to retention in grade.

In a similar vein, Samuels (2006) rejected the claims that DIBELS did a good job of predicting reading achievement as measured on traditional standardized assessments. He noted, for instance, that the studies reporting a strong relationship between DIBELS oral reading rate and accuracy scores and reading comprehension were fundamentally flawed—flawed because the estimates of comprehension were not done on the DIBELS materials that the students read but on other tests given at a later time. Thus, on the DIBELS assessment, students could read fast and not worry about comprehension. However, with no reliable test of comprehension after the fast DIBELS reading, there are no data to indicate whether fast reading is linked to better understanding.

The studies reviewed by Walczyk and Griffith-Ross (2007) suggest otherwise. They report that the first strategic adaptation that good readers use when they confront comprehension difficulties is to slow down their rate of reading. The next most common adaptation is to reread the confusing sentence. If readers do either of these while taking the DIBELS tests, their scores will plummet. In other words, DIBELS scoring guidelines penalize readers for engaging in the very fix-up strategies that good readers use.

Finally, in an analysis of research that appears on the DIBELS website, Wilde (2006) noted that although all the numbers look impressive, there are real problems for making instructional decisions with DIBELS data:

> If this DIBELS test were used to decide which students should receive extra instruction, schools would have to determine whether to help just the "high-risk" students or the "some-risk" ones as well. There were 361 students who didn't meet the state benchmark; only half of them (178) would have gotten extra help if it only went to those in the "high-risk" category. If help were given to the "high-risk" and "some-risk" categories, it would catch most of those likely to not meet benchmark (308), but extra help would also be given to 230 students who didn't need it. (p. 67)

Independent researchers examining the reliability of DIBELS for making judgments about reading development have demonstrated the inadequacy of this test. What DIBELS does do reasonably well is identify the readers making very little progress toward reading fluency. As for higher-achieving readers, DIBELS misidentifies far too many children as making adequate progress who are not and identifies too many children as at-risk when they are not.

Mathson, Solic, and Allington (2006) reported a small study of the reliability of DIBELS with third-grade readers. The data in Table 4.1 are drawn from that study and illustrate how widely variable performances on the DIBELS Oral Reading Fluency subtest can be. These data illustrate the DIBELS words correct per minute (wcpm) scores of 10 students in the analysis. Each student read three DIBELS passages aloud on the same day, passages of equivalent difficulty according to the DIBELS manual. Examine the "variability" column that shows the difference between the fastest and slowest reading each student did on the day they were tested.

▶ Table 4.1 **Variability in DIBELS Oral Reading Fluency performances**

	Passages numbered			
Student #	**1**	**2**	**3**	**Variability in wcpm**
S4	118	81	71	47
S13	66	38	46	28
S14	92	60	69	32
S25	90	73	54	36
S30	94	79	45	49
S31	165	128	109	56
S32	97	64	69	33
S34	80	66	47	33
S35	74	44	35	39
S38	81	52	58	29

Altwerger, Jordan, and Shelton (2008) report findings almost identical to our study and they further found that standardized assessments of word reading did not predict DIBELS fluency scores well. The fastest readers on the DIBELS ORF assessment had word recognition scores between the 17th and 99th percentiles on the Woodcock-Johnson reading assessment. How can any test that produces this much variation in performance be considered reliable? It can only if you discard two-thirds of the data, which is precisely what the DIBELS manual directs teachers to do. In other words, one way to attempt to make the DIBELS tests look more reliable than they are involves tossing out the fastest and slowest performances. But which of the three rates is really the right one—the one that best portrays students' typical speed and accuracy performances?

The authors (Mathson, Solic, & Allington, 2006) also computed the correlation between the three DIBELS scores each student achieved. Basically, these readers fell into three distinct groups as a result of this analysis. For one group ($n = 11$) the reliability of the DIBELS reading rate and accuracy was below $r = .25$. This means that their performances varied widely from passage to passage. Another group ($n = 16$) had scores that had correlations between .25 and .50. For these readers, DIBELS reading rate and accuracy again varied quite a bit. The third group ($n = 12$) had correlations above .50, still not very high but higher than the other groups.

What should you make of this analysis? The authors' interpretation is that DIBELS does not measure reading rate and accuracy with any reliability. The variation from one passage to another is simply so large that even using just the middle range score is likely to misinform teachers about students' development.

Now all of this may seem a bit picky and a lot technical. But given the time, cost, and energy it takes to administer the DIBELS assessments regularly, I think we should expect a better test. If the DIBELS developers and promoters could provide evidence of what has been dubbed "consequential validity," then I would be willing to modify my stance. But there are no such data. Basically, a study of the consequential validity of DIBELS would require a demonstration that when schools use the DIBELS assessments, instruction improves as well as achievement. But to identify DIBELS as the reason scores improved would require a randomized experiment where a number of schools used the same core reading program, and in some of those schools, but not all, DIBELS was randomly assigned to also be used to make instructional decisions. If the reading achievement of the schools using DIBELS then improved more than the scores in the schools using the same core program but not using DIBELS, then I might be satisfied that DIBELS is not simply a time-consuming fraud.

I won't hold my breath until the developers conduct such a study, but I will continue to point out that there is no evidence that using DIBELS produces better teaching or learning.

Why Is DIBELS Used in So Many Schools?

How is it that DIBELS has become the most widely used assessment in schools intending to monitor fluency development? The short answer to this question is: powerful political connections and a hint of entrepreneurial corruption. As noted by the Office of the Inspector General (2006) of the U.S. Department of Education and in the Congressional hearings on the Reading

First component of the NCLB (Glenn, 2007), various federally linked consultants promoted the use of DIBELS to state education agencies, and a contested review of the adequacy of various reading assessments, including DIBELS, was purposely positioned on the Reading First website to make it appear it had some official endorsement by the USDE. It did not.

> For a series of articles reporting on these problems in the Reading First program, visit **www.edweek.org/ew/collections/reading-first/index.html**.

In the end, the majority of states included DIBELS as the primary tool for monitoring fluency development and reading progress. Officials from several states testified that they were told by the then director of the federal Reading First office that the state's Reading First application would not be approved unless DIBELS was the preferred assessment tool (Brownstein & Hicks, 2006). After the state education agency identified DIBELS as the preferred monitoring assessment, school districts participating in the Reading First program then were required to use DIBELS. Thus, DIBELS became a commercial success not because of its unique technical qualities but because of entrepreneurial manipulation. The millions of dollars in earnings that DIBELS delivers have the developers and publishers smiling all the way to the bank.

Before moving on, I must also note that DIBELS is now being used in many schools that do not participate in the Reading First program. These schools elected to use DIBELS. Why? I cannot explain these decisions and will also suggest that given the research available, school personnel would be hard pressed to defend their decisions on scientific grounds. What I think the widespread nonmandated use of DIBELS suggests is that educational faddism is still alive and prospering. Most worrisome is that in too many school systems DIBELS is being used as the progress monitoring tool in response to intervention (RTI) initiatives. However, the research on DIBELS is such that anyone using DIBELS to make important decisions about students' development of reading proficiencies is guilty of educational malpractice.

If Not DIBELS, What?

The truth of the matter is that if schools want to monitor the rate and accuracy of students' oral reading, there are several well-known techniques for doing so. In fact, DIBELS was an attempt to use a somewhat similar technique but to generate earnings as well. Both the words correct per minute technique (Deno, 1985) and the running records technique (Johnston, 2000) provide rate and accuracy data just as DIBELS does.

The advantage of both of these well-known techniques, besides the no-cost feature, is that both assess student progress on the curriculum materials they use every day—in other words, they are curriculum-based data. If teachers want information on whether instruction needs to be modified, then data gathered from student responses while reading the texts that are being used for instruction are far more useful than scores from random and specially written passages such as those found in the DIBELS assessment.

For instance, I've noted that one critical feature of reading lessons is ensuring that students have books of appropriate difficulty in their hands. Using curriculum-based measures of rate, accuracy, fluency, and comprehension can tell you whether you are using the right texts. Data from random texts cannot provide that critical bit of information.

If, for some reason, you wanted to assess the acquisition of certain decoding skills using a sample of non-words, then using non-words that are constructed of the phonic elements that have been taught will provide better information than a test that includes non-words with elements that have not yet been taught (which is the case with the DIBELS non-word fluency subtest and many other decoding tests).

Like Sandra Wilde (2006), I suppose I could see the DIBELS assessment being used as an initial screening device—as a crude but quick tool to identify which students seem to be in trouble with reading acquisition. But given how crudely it measures subskills, I wonder whether schools (and children) might not be better served by using either of the curriculum-based assessment techniques. In the end, the evidence for the power of curriculum-based measurements to improve instruction is too compelling to ignore. The NRP (2000) agreed and noted that a number of procedures might be used to assess and monitor oral reading fluency (pp. 3–9). These included running records, words correct per minute calculations, miscue analysis, informal reading inventories, standardized oral reading assessments, and pausing indices. I will discuss the first two procedures next.

☆ Curriculum-Based Measurement of Fluency

Curriculum-based measurement offers a number of advantages that make these sorts of assessments instructionally useful. One key finding is that when schools adopt curriculum-based measurement techniques, both teaching and learning improves (see Deno & Marston, 2006, for a review).

As you listen to readers who struggle with fluency you should be asking yourself this question: Why is this reader having fluency problems? Is it because:

_____ He doesn't recognize many high-frequency words at a glance?

_____ She decodes lots of words slowly, letter by letter?

_____ He seems to be missing decoding skills appropriate for his reading level?

_____ She waits for adult help rather than attempt unknown words independently?

_____ He doesn't know the meanings of many words he is trying to read?

_____ She doesn't pay attention to punctuation?

_____ He is not self-monitoring while reading?

_____ She is trying to read fast and not attending to understanding?

_____ He seems anxious and uncomfortable reading aloud?

_____ She is remarkably better in accuracy, rate, and fluency if I allow her to read the text silently before she reads aloud?

Teachers can use these measures to monitor growth and progress of students in the curricular materials students use every day. When gathering such data repeatedly, teachers use the data for individuals and track progress toward peer-referenced or other normative standards. I've mentioned two well-known examples, running records and words correct per minute. In the following section each of these techniques will be developed in greater detail. In addition, since neither technique originally evaluated fluency, I provide guidelines for complementing the rate and accuracy data with a rating of fluency.

Running Records

Peter Johnston (2000) has written a small book that details the development of running records and the research on this technique that originated with Marie Clay (1985). Johnston includes detailed guidelines on how data are collected using the running record technique and provides an audiotape for developing proficiency using running records to inform instruction. If you are unfamiliar with the running record technique for recording oral reading performances but plan to use this approach, I'd suggest getting a copy of Johnston's book even though I outline the procedure here.

It is important to understand that in this section I am not providing the full running record process. Instead, I am recommending that the *technique* used in recording reading behaviors be implemented in assessing and monitoring oral reading performance. As a matter of fact, I am not even providing all the coding features used in the running records process, because you can use the technique to collect useful evidence even without the full complement of codes.

Using the running record technique to gather data on student performance in the curriculum materials used in the reading instruction requires virtually nothing but a pencil and a clean sheet of lined notebook paper. The advantage of this is that running records can be collected with very little preparation. In fact, if you always have a notebook of lined paper, a pencil, and timer handy when you work with students, there would be no preparation required. Thus, unlike techniques that require that you photocopy the text the student will read to you or require that you locate the packet of assessment materials that will be used, the running record can be done literally spontaneously.

Following the basic procedures for gathering running record data, you would select a text that is used in the daily reading lessons but one the student has not yet read. Typically, you would have the reader begin at the beginning of the selection and read through it. If the selection is long, you might decide to have the student read only some portion of the text.

When the reader begins, you note the time or start a stopwatch. When the reader has finished, you note the time or turn off the stopwatch and record the time spent reading. As the reader reads aloud, you simply make a check mark on the lined sheet of paper for every word pronounced correctly. For words that are mispronounced, you write a dash. On the blank sheet of lined paper, then, you would have a record that looked like this for a five-word sentence where one word was mispronounced: ✓✓✓ — ✓. If the reader skipped over a word, you write an O (for omitted) and the record would look like this: ✓✓ O ✓✓. It is important to remember that if a misread word is self-corrected—read correctly—then you count that word as correctly identified. The feature box below provides the other symbols you will need to create the running record of oral reading behaviors.

After the child has completed the oral reading assessment, you need to take a minute (literally) and calculate accuracy and rate of reading and fluency. To figure the accuracy level, divide the number of words read incorrectly

Commonly Used Running Record Symbols

Correct response	✓	✓✓✓✓✓✓
Misread word	—	✓✓—✓✓✓✓
Omission	O	✓✓✓✓ O✓✓
Insertion	^	✓✓✓✓ ^ ✓✓
Teacher prompt	T	✓✓✓ T✓✓✓✓

or omitted by the total number of words read (for example, 5 words read inaccurately in a 121-word text results in a 4 percent error rate, or a 96 percent accuracy level). To calculate reading rate, simply divide the total time spent reading by the total number of words read (if the reader took 2 minutes and 12 seconds to read a 121-word passage, the reading rate would be 55 words per minute). One advantage of measuring reading in one-minute segments is that it makes calculating reading rate much easier.

Recording the reader's level of fluency would be the next step (details on fluency ratings appear later in this chapter). The full running record procedure also includes evaluating the nature of the errors readers make to draw inferences about the strategies being used and not being used. But you will need to study Johnston's book to add that level of analysis to your toolbox.

You can use both oral reading accuracy and rate data to monitor a reader's progress. Additionally, the accuracy data can be used to determine whether the classroom text that the reader read from is of an appropriate level of difficulty for instructional use.

Words Correct per Minute (wcpm)

Shinn (1989) provides a detailed account of how to gather and use wcpm data to monitor oral reading development, and interested readers should study his text to develop a fuller understanding of the method. The traditional wcpm technique has readers read aloud for one minute from materials used in their reading lessons. Typically, the teacher makes a photocopy of the text to be read and then, as the child reads, simply crosses out any word read incorrectly. When the reading is completed, you simply count the number of correctly read words to calculate wcpm data. This number is recorded and typically entered on a graph that is used to track changes in rate and accuracy of oral reading. By tracking a reader's wcpm, you can observe whether progress is being made in terms of faster and more accurate reading of instructional texts. As with the running record technique, you can also evaluate the appropriateness of the difficulty of a text for instructional purposes. An example of a sequence of graphed wcpm data is displayed in Figure 4.1.

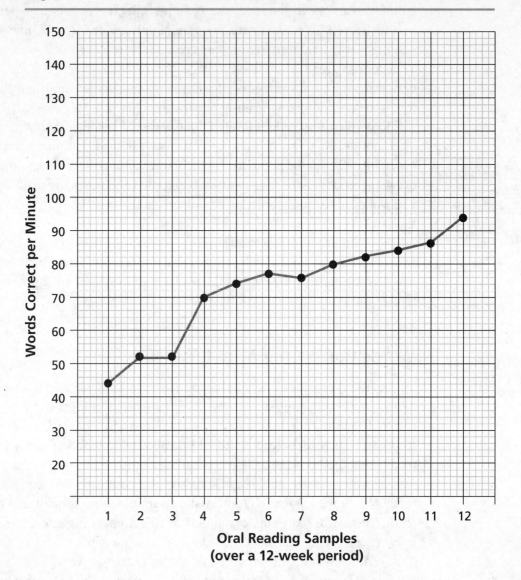

Judging the Adequacy of a Student's Oral Reading Rate

Graphing wcpm or rate and accuracy data is a good start, but how do you interpret such data? If you gather repeated samples of oral reading over time (say, one semester), you will probably be able to see whether improvement is being made. I say "probably" because to assess progress on wcpm, you would need to ensure the texts used in the several samples were of similar difficulty. It may be naïve to think that samples from the same core reading program are of equal difficulty. However, using one-minute oral reading samples means that you could use a single story from later in the reader to gather all of your samples. Alternatively, you could use a single book from the classroom library to gather the growth samples.

If one goal is using oral reading wcpm to evaluate the appropriateness of the text for instructional purposes, then the data should be gathered on those texts. Likewise, if you are interested in evaluating a student's success in the curriculum materials you are using, you would also gather the wcpm data from the curriculum materials in use.

The best data on average grade-level oral reading wcpm levels can be found in Table 4.2. These data come from a study of over 200,000 students in 23 states. The table displays the average wcpm at three times each year (no data for fall of grade 1 are provided because many students have not begun to read at that point). The average wcpm data can help you see how any particular student in your class compares to most other students at his or her grade level at different times during the school year. But these are "average" wcpm data, with half of the students reading faster and slower than the numbers displayed. If you are interested in information on oral reading rates that fall in the average range (as opposed to exactly average) go to www.prel.org/products/re_/assessingfluency.pdf to find an excellent brief written by Tim Rasinski that includes those data.

Note that wcpm data for the spring of grades 6, 7, and 8 do not vary. In other words, the typical student shows no growth over the three years of middle school! It isn't that 150 wcpm is the uppermost level that can be achieved, because the top 10 percent of grade 5, as well as grade 6, 7, and 8, students read at the 200 wcpm level or faster. These wcpm data indicate

► Table 4.2 **Average wcpm oral reading performances by grade level and time of year**

	Fall	Winter	Spring
Grade 1		23	53
Grade 2	51	72	89
Grade 3	71	92	107
Grade 4	94	112	123
Grade 5	110	127	139
Grade 6	127	140	150
Grade 7	128	136	150
Grade 8	133	146	151

Source: Hasbrouck & Tindal, 2006.

what lots of other data on middle school reading achievement indicate—at the present time, middle school instruction does not foster much reading growth.

Additional Considerations

I worry that when teachers collect oral reading data cold, those situations where the reader has never seen the text before, teachers might get data that do not truly reflect what the reader would do normally when reading. Oral reading is different from silent reading, if only in the public performance aspect. It has been my experience that some, maybe many, readers experience a bit of anxiety when asked to read aloud, especially in settings where their peers can hear them. But even if anxiety isn't particularly high, I still think asking readers to read aloud may alter their use of reading strategies.

For instance, researchers know that proficient readers slow down their reading when they encounter difficulty. Proficient readers also reread sections that are confusing. But these powerful and productive fix-up strategies may be suppressed when students read aloud. Likewise, sounding out an unknown word is another useful strategy that proficient readers use but perhaps use less often when reading aloud because it sounds bad and slows down reading. In some readers' minds, it may be better just to guess and go on reading aloud.

Finally, the very presence of you, the teacher, may alter what the reader does. In independent silent reading you are not available nor are you monitoring the reading. So maybe in this case the reader will elect just to skip over an unknown word the first time she or he encounters it ("I think I'll skip over it because my reading experience tells me that if this is an important word, I'll likely see it again in the story"). But when the reader is reading aloud to you, the reader may try to get you to support his or her efforts. This is precisely what McGill-Franzen and McDermott (1978) reported. The very presence of the teacher altered the reading strategies the reader used. And once assistance was given, the reader more frequently requested assistance. Why not take advantage of having the teacher right there beside you?

So, ask yourself, "Does this reader's oral reading seem to reflect what I know about him or her as a reader?" If you have questions about a student's cold oral reading data, I have two alternatives to suggest.

Reading Cold versus Reading Previously Read Text

First, it might be useful to collect running records data on curriculum-based passages read cold and again on curriculum materials the reader has had a chance to read silently before reading aloud. It seems to me that if you see a dramatic difference between the two reading samples, you need to reflect on just what you want to learn about the reader's development.

For instance, as commonly seems to occur, an oral reading of a text after having first read it silently produces a different reading record. Often there are fewer errors, hesitations, and self-corrections, and better fluency when the text has been previously read silently. So what might this tell you about the reader? I think the oral rereading provides the best case scenario. It demonstrates that the reader has successfully employed a variety of strategies to read the text accurately and fluently. What I worry about is that if you collect only oral reading data cold, you might underestimate the use of powerful strategies that the reader normally uses.

And what if the silent prereading produces no observable changes in rate, accuracy, or fluency? In this case it seems that what you see when the reader reads a text cold is what you would see if we could somehow observe his or her silent reading processes. But when large differences are observed in rate, accuracy, and fluency when the text is read cold or read after silent reading, I think you should consider that the cold oral reading performance is at odds with the typical way the reader reads.

Over the years I've encountered some children who have quite discrepant scores when I compare cold reading versus rereading of a text. Some readers seem to find the cold oral reading of a text intimidating and so rush through it, just to be over with it. Having the opportunity to read the selection silently prior to the oral rendition works to ameliorate the intimidation factor and produces evidence of better reading abilities than one would have expected from the cold oral reading alone.

Allowing a Running Start Before Gathering Oral Reading Data

I will suggest another alternative that also seems potentially useful in improving the reliability of cold oral reading records. This involves allowing the reader to read a bit of the text aloud before beginning to collect the oral reading record data. If you are using the core reading program anthology or a leveled book to gather the curriculum-based oral reading data, you simply allow the reader to read the first few paragraphs (or pages) before you begin to gather your one-minute sample.

This modification allows the reader to become familiar with the story and perhaps get into the flow of reading aloud. This alternative does not go against the traditional grain of oral reading assessment procedures but it does provide the reader with a type of support that is unavailable in the typical oral reading assessment.

Audiotape Recording the Oral Reading Session

Years ago I compared teachers' scoring of oral reading behavior with audiotaped recordings of those same reading performances. What I found was that, generally speaking, teachers were typically not very accurate at scoring oral reading while the reader was reading. This continues to worry me today. So, following Johnston's (1991) advice, I will suggest that as you learn to use the running records or wcpm techniques, you initially tape record the student's reading and check on the accuracy of your coding. Do the same with ratings of fluency. Once you are satisfied that you are recording reading behaviors accurately, you can stop taping. You might want to recheck your accuracy every once in awhile (say twice a year), but taping creates more preparation and uses twice as much time as recording oral reading live.

Assessing the Size of the At-a-Glance Vocabulary

One final assessment that may be useful is examining how many words the struggling reader knows at a glance. There are two basic strategies: One is a contextualized assessment done while the student is reading aloud from a text and the other is a test of recognition in isolation. For the contextualized assessment, you simply examine your running record or wcpm data. Note how many high-frequency words were misread or omitted. This analysis lets you see whether virtually all high-frequency words were read accurately.

You might also want to assess the recognition of the high-frequency words in isolation (and maybe even compare the reader's accuracy in isolation to his or her accuracy in context). To do this you need to assess in a way that does not allow the student unlimited time to examine the word and respond. The simplest technique I've found for this is to write the words to be assessed on 3" × 5" cards (or type or print them using a 16- to 20-point font size). The most common source for high-frequency words is the Dolch list of 220 common words (see Appendix B) but there are other lists that you could use. To ensure that this assessment is curriculum-based, check that any word you assess is found in the reading materials being used.

Once you have a list of the words you want to check to see if they are recognized at a glance and have printed those words on cards, you are ready to begin the assessment. Shuffle the word cards and then place a blank 3" × 5" card as the first card. You will use this blank card to "flash" each word to the student. Tell the student you are going to show him a word for just a second and then uncover the word. He should try to say the word as soon as he

knows it. You then proceed through the deck of word cards, one at a time. You simply slide the blank card up and then down, exposing the word on the second card very briefly. You might begin sliding the card up and down more slowly then pick up the speed, thus shortening the exposure. You can simply place any card with a word the student does not pronounce correctly in one pile and the words correctly identified in another. Later you can complete a record form indicating which words seem to be consistently and quickly recognized after a brief exposure and which still present difficulties.

Assessing the recognition of function words in isolation (on flashcards or word lists) makes the task more difficult than assessing recognition in the context of oral reading of a text. An alternative, then, is to identify the high-frequency function words in the passages a reader read during the wcpm assessment. In other words, analyze the accuracy of identification of function words in those passages as an optional or additional assessment. You could simply list the function words and note whether each was correctly identified when reading the wcpm passages aloud. I've found that some struggling readers seem to achieve higher recognition scores when reading a passage than when these words are assessed in isolation.

It is important that readers have a large store of words they recognize at a glance. It is also important that the number of at-a-glance words keeps growing if fluent reading is the goal. At every grade level the best readers add more words to their at-a-glance word bank so that by adulthood the vast majority of words a person encounters are read at a glance with little cognitive effort. This is the key to reading fluently with expression and comprehension.

Assessing Comprehension

Remember that the definition of fluency includes the ability to demonstrate an understanding of the text that was read. So how do you best assess student understanding after reading? I suggest that a global comprehension rating of a retelling of the text content is perhaps the most reliable and most efficient strategy for evaluating student comprehension after reading. This is an individual assessment, but because fluency measures are also individual assessments this technique seems appropriate. Retelling assessments involve you asking the student to recall everything she or he remembers about the text that she or he just read. You then compare the text content to what the student told you and then rate comprehension as good, fair, or poor. Figure 4.2 provides guidelines for each of these ratings.

If you want to make this evaluation more formalized, you can use the scoring strategy that Pressley, Hilden, and Shankland (2005) used. This strategy is similar to the comprehension assessment found in the Durrell Analysis of Reading Difficulties (Durrell, 1955). Here are the guidelines for scoring retellings using an "idea unit" analysis.

Idea unit analysis has been long used by researchers as a measure of comprehension, although it is primarily a measure of recall. The basic notion is to examine the retelling to see how many of the ideas in the passage were included in the retelling. Idea units can be understood as phrases in the passage. So, to develop a retelling scoring guide you would first break the text down into phrases. Next, print the phrases in order as illustrated on page 70. As the student does the retelling, simply put a check mark next to each idea/phrase that is recalled. After the student finishes the retelling, ask, "Is there anything more that you remember?" If more information is now recalled, place check marks next to those phrases. Now count the number of recalled idea units and compare that to the total number. You could convert this into a percentage and use that as your score for the retell.

Although this percentage could be used as the score, it does not exactly represent a "comprehension" score as one normally uses it. That's because to earn a 100 percent score the reader would have to retell every bit of the passage, including even small details. But in normal reading, people often forget details but recall the gist of texts they've read. So I suggest that you use the percentage and graph it and use it to monitor comprehension but do not get worried if the percentage hovers around 60 percent rather 100 percent.

▶ Figure 4.2 **Retelling global comprehension scoring guidelines**

Good: Recalls most of the important ideas in the text that was read.

Fair: Recalls some of the ideas but omits some details as well.

Poor: Recalls few ideas from the text.

This passage has been broken down into idea/phrase units for scoring a retelling.

> I couldn't do my homework.
> I was thinking about what to say /
> to Michael tomorrow.
> There had to be a million mean things /
> to say to him.
> But I was so mad /
> I couldn't think of any.

Source: Bill Cosby, *The Meanest Things to Say* (New York: Scholastic, 1997).

⭐ Evaluating Fluency and Its Development

In this final section I offer a powerful procedure for monitoring oral reading fluency. Fluency evaluations should always be part and parcel of every evaluation of oral reading proficiencies.

There are several fluency rating schemes including a couple I've developed (Allington, 2006b; Allington & Brown, 1979), but I think the preferred fluency rating scale is the one used in the fluency evaluations (Daane et al., 2005; Pinnell et al., 1995) as part of the National Assessment of Educational Progress (NAEP). Both research teams used a four-point fluency scale (see Figure 4.3) to portray the status of fluency development among fourth-grade students. In both studies, fluency ratings were strongly linked to reading comprehension performance. They also found that approximately 60 percent of the students achieved Level 3 or 4 on the fluency scale. These students read with 96 percent accuracy on average. The average reading rate was 119 words per minute. Almost all students reading at Levels 1 and 2 on the scale fell below the basic reading proficiency standard on the NAEP and read more slowly with an average of 94 percent accuracy.

To monitor fluency development, you simply include a numerical rating of fluency every time you gather data using either the running record or wcpm technique. In addition to charting rate and accuracy or wcpm performances of each reader, you also chart the fluency rating (see Figure 4.4). Appendix A includes several forms useful for recording these data. Forms for individuals and a class record are necessary for monitoring.

As you evaluate student oral reading fluency, remember that it is quite common that first-graders are still stuck to the print. Thus, on cold readings of text you should expect a Level 1 or 2 rating. It is typically in second grade when readers begin to get unstuck. But honestly, it is not uncommon for many readers to be in the upper elementary grades before they can read a text cold at Level 3 or 4. Having younger students practice a text (you model fluent reading and they reread the text several times attempting to emulate

▶ Figure 4.3   **NAEP four-point fluency scale**

Level 4:   Reads primarily in larger, meaningful phrase groups. Although some regressions, repetitions, and deviations from the text may be present, those do not appear to detract from the overall structure of the story. Preservation of the author's syntax is consistent. Some or most of the story is read with expressive interpretation.

Level 3:   Reads primarily in three- or four-word phrase groups. Some smaller groupings may be present. However, the majority of phrasing seems appropriate and preserves the syntax of the author. Little or no expressive interpretation is present.

Level 2:   Reads primarily in two-word phrases with some three- and four-word groupings. Some word-by-word reading may be present. Word groupings may seem awkward and unrelated to larger context of sentence or passage.

Level 1:   Reads primarily word-by-word. Occasionally two- or three-word phrases may occur, but these are infrequent and/or do not preserve meaningful syntax.

Source: Pinnell et al., 1995.

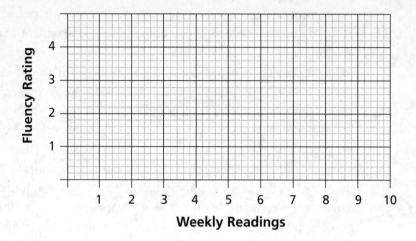

▶ Figure 4.4 **Fluency graphing**

your performance) until they are achieving Level 3 and 4 ratings is also useful because it helps them see, hear, and feel what fluent reading is like. My point is that it is unreasonable to expect high levels of fluency when reading texts cold until students develop some advanced reading proficiencies.

Finally, it is important that when working with struggling readers you select rate, accuracy, wcpm, and fluency targets that match their reading level rather than their grade level. A critical first step in accelerating reading development is to help the reader exhibit performances that mirror good readers at his or her reading level. In other words, you work to turn the struggling reader into a good reader at the level he or she is currently at before moving the child into more difficult materials and expecting mastery of more complex skills and strategies.

Technology Applications for Recording Running Record and wcpm Data

Wireless Generation (www.wirelessgeneration.com/products.php?prod= mClass:Reading) produces the handheld personal digital assistants (PDAs) that many schools use for gathering and graphing DIBELS data and sells software for digital recording of running record and wcpm data. This reading record software built into the PDA allows you to simply tap words misread,

Monitoring Students' Reading Development

When it comes to monitoring the development of student reading proficiencies we have two different but related schemes for doing so that have experimental research supporting their use. Ross (2004) compared the quality of reading instruction offered and student achievement for two groups of teachers. One group had been trained in the running record data-gathering scheme and the other group of teachers received no such training. The teachers who used the running records technique provided higher-quality lessons, and student achievement was significantly higher than the achievement of students in the control classroom where the technique was not used. Fuchs, Deno, and Mirkin (1984) report on a similar study with similar outcomes but here the one group of teachers received training in using the wcpm technique for monitoring reading development. Again, both teaching and learning were better in the classrooms of teachers who used that technique.

In both studies some teachers learned a strategy for monitoring student performance in the curriculum materials used during their reading lessons. Both focused teachers' attention on reading accuracy and reading rate. Just a small amount of training on either technique improved the reading instruction offered and this led to improved reading achievement.

omitted, self-corrected, repeated, and so on. As soon as the student is finished, the software calculates accuracy, wcpm, and self-correction rate and enters the data in both a student record and a class record file. It also updates the graphs showing previous performances. For those teachers who know how to complete a full analysis of the running records data, the software allows the analysis of the errors and then charts that performance as well.

The Wireless Generation software also currently includes an electronic file of over 3,000 leveled books from a dozen or so educational publishers (e.g., National Geographic, Newbridge, Heinemann, Mondo, Wright Group, and others). Teachers can call up any of these texts for scoring a student's read-aloud. However, none of the publishers of core reading programs currently allows Wireless Generation to display the stories included in their

readers. Thus, the use of this assessment tool is limited to schools that use a leveled books approach rather than a core reading program, since you need to track progress in the curriculum materials students are using. A final limitation of this product is that it confuses wcpm with a fluency assessment. No fluency scale is included on the software.

> Other technology-based tools for developing curriculum-based measurement graphs and class profiles of oral reading performance data are available at no cost at www.interventioncentral.com.

★ Summary

Gathering data on student's oral reading performances is one powerful way to monitor progress and to access data that are useful for adapting reading lessons. Perhaps because there has been a widespread mislabeling of reading rate and accuracy assessments as "fluency" assessments, much of the research and development has been conducted on gathering and using rate and accuracy records to monitor progress and inform instruction. Both the running records technique and the wcpm procedure provide oral reading rate and accuracy data but neither have traditionally provided data on fluency.

Techniques for gathering rate, accuracy, and at-a-glance word data have been detailed in this chapter along with a simple four-point fluency scale used in the National Assessment of Educational Progress. Although other fluency scales are available, the NAEP fluency scale is relatively straightforward and requires little training to use.

Monitoring fluency development is important, but if the assessments find that some readers seem to be in trouble, then instruction must be adapted to address those difficulties. Only when the assessment data produce positive changes in reading instruction can one say that the time spent in assessment was worthwhile. The next chapter discusses how instruction might be adapted and modified when not every student is developing as a proficient reader.

chapter 5

Fostering the Development of Fluent Readers in Core Reading Lessons

At this point you should have a good understanding of how fluency typically develops and why some students seem to struggle in developing fluent reading.

In this chapter I take everything we have covered thus far and focus on how to create reading lessons that better foster fluency in the classroom, especially for beginning readers. The discussion focuses on modifications and adaptations to the typical classroom reading lesson.

☆ Classroom Reading Lessons that Foster Fluency

Teachers can create classroom reading lessons that do a better job at fostering fluency development. In doing so, teachers can substantially reduce the number of beginning readers who struggle to acquire oral fluency and the number of readers who never seem to develop into fluent readers. In this chapter, then, I describe the five types of modifications and adaptations to the typical classroom reading lesson that will need to be made to better support the development of reading fluency in all readers.

Access to High-Success Texts

As detailed in the earlier chapters, reading development is best fostered when students have "just right" texts in their hands all day long. High-success texts are critical. High-success texts for fluency lessons and practice are texts that can be read with 99 percent accuracy, and they are critical for fostering fluency development.

Several modifications of the traditional reading lesson commonly found in core reading programs can convert those texts into high-success texts and make them appropriate for fluency lessons. The first modification is adding a shared book experience (SBE) component to the standard lesson, especially when fluency is the goal. Research supports the use of the SBE to foster improved word recognition, necessary for reading with at least 99 percent accuracy (Rasinski & Hoffman, 2003; Reutzel, Eldredge, & Hollingsworth, 1994). The SBE adaptation simply has the teacher read the text to be used in the lesson aloud to students as they follow along. Then the text might be read aloud chorally, with the teacher leading the reading. Remember that the SBE includes several other opportunities for rereading the text in group choral rereadings, paired readings with a classmate, and so on.

Note that not all core reading programs have lesson designs that are easily adapted. In addition, the texts presented for students to read typically vary across several levels of difficulty (Hiebert, 2002; McGill-Franzen et al., 2006). Thus, fostering fluency using core reading program materials may be problematic and you may want to consider simply adding a separate fluency component to the reading lesson.

One alternative is the fluency development lesson (FDL). The FDL is a 15-minute daily add-on to the regular reading instruction lesson (Rasinski & Hoffman, 2003). Here, students read and reread high-success texts, often a poem or rhythmic texts. The initial reading is by the teacher, followed by several choral readings of the same passage with the teacher. After a short discussion of the text, the students practice rereading the text three times each with a classmate. At this point the students perform the passage for the class.

Another problem commonly found in core reading program materials was discussed earlier: the presence of a large number of infrequently used words along with the limited repetition of many words (Hiebert & Fisher, 2005). Thus, it may be best to consider using different texts in a FDL or any other lessons focused on developing fluency specifically.

Alter Patterns of Responses to Reading Errors

Providing all students with daily access to high-success texts to read will hopefully produce a positive effect on the rate and nature of the teacher interruptions when students, especially struggling readers, are reading aloud. As I documented in Chapter 3, teachers currently interrupt their weaker readers more often and more quickly, and when they interrupt, they rarely direct the reader's attention to self-monitoring of reading. But if all readers are placed in high-success texts, then fewer interruptions should be one positive result.

Nonetheless, teachers will still need to modify their interruption behaviors even when only 1 word in every 100 is misread. I've argued that the "pause-prompt-praise" strategy seems the most appropriate modification (Allington, 2006b). Very simply, the first step in this strategy is to "pause," to wait a few seconds after a reader misreads. Even a three-second pause would be a great improvement. This may require the teacher to adopt a "one thousand one, one thousand two, one thousand three" silent counting approach. The goal is to allow the reader time to notice the misreading, to engage in a fix-up strategy, and then to self-correct without prompting from the teacher (or peers). If the three-second pause does not lead to a self-correction, then the teacher provides a prompt, but what sort of prompt depends on both the type of misreading and the reader's skills and prior knowledge. For instance, a prompt such as, "Sound it out" after a student has misread *tongue* as /tahn goo/ would make no sense, since the misread indicates the student already tried sounding out unsuccessfully. In such a case it might make sense to prompt, "Does that make sense?" but only if the word *tongue* is familiar and used in a common context. It also might make sense to prompt, "Just read on," especially if later in the text the word is more richly context-ualized. Finally, the teacher could simply prompt with the correct pronuncia-tion and then ask the reader to reread from the beginning of the sentence in which the misread occurred.

If, during the three-second pause, the reader does figure out the word, praise the self-correction strategy and any other strategy use that is observed. In fact, I suggest that after the reading is completed you return to locations in the text where self-corrections occurred and have the reader recall what happened and again praise the strategy use.

Modeling Fluent Reading

One reason why the SBE and the FDL have been shown to be successful is undoubtedly the fact that both provide readers with a model of what fluent reading sounds like. Modeling of fluent reading is another modification to the typical reading lesson that is important, especially if some students seem to have had few opportunities to hear fluent reading.

A daily read-aloud from children's books can also work to provide mod-els of what fluent reading sounds like. In addition, there are lots of other good reasons to read aloud every day, including familiarizing students with various genres of text, fostering growth in listening vocabulary, and initiating literate conversations about the text being read. Research supports the positive effects of reading aloud in each of these areas (Trelease, 2001).

Some commercial products are available that provide taped readings of texts. The problem with many of these materials is that the reader on the tape is a professional reader, and the reading is done too quickly. In other words, often students cannot keep up with the pace of the taped reading and so simply sit and listen to the tape. Listening to a good story on tape has some merits, but it is not the same as following along with a fluent reader model. Thus, if you plan to use taped recordings of texts to supply the fluent reading model, I suggest that you create the tapes and work to ensure that while you read in phrases with expression, you also read a bit less quickly than you might in a typical read-aloud situation.

Repeated Readings

As the NRP noted after reviewing the research on fluency, there have been numerous studies supporting the rereading of texts as an intervention that fosters fluency and accuracy. Again, the demonstrated benefits of the SBE and FDL seem linked to the fact that both have the students read and reread the texts used in those lesson models. Repeated readings work best when the students have been provided a model of a fluent reading of the text and when support, at least initially, is available, often in the form of choral reading or assisted reading support.

Repeated readings produce the most powerful effects when students are rereading high-success texts and when they are monitoring their reading rate and fluency using some evaluative process. This may entail charting their reading rate and accuracy and estimating their fluency rating. Providing students with targets for rate, accuracy, and fluency has also been shown to enhance the likelihood that repeated readings produce positive effects.

One motivational method for producing repeated readings of texts is reader's theater (Worthy & Prater, 2002). Several studies have demonstrated the positive impact of reader's theater on fluency and accuracy and on students' motivation to engage in repeated readings (Griffith & Rasinski, 2004; Martinez et al., 1999; Worthy, Broaddus, & Ivey, 2001). The basic method is to locate texts that can be dramatically reenacted. Many core reading programs, for instance, provide scripts that can be used, and there are website resources that do the same (see Figure 5.1 for web resources). Having scripts makes it rather easy to develop a reader's theater production, but remember that the scripts themselves need to be high-success texts.

My preferred alternative to prepared scripts is to have the students themselves select a portion of text to prepare as a script. Texts that have lots of dialogue are ideal for this purpose. For instance, the *Frog and Toad* series by

▶ Figure 5.1   **Websites for reader's theater resources**

www.readingonline.org/electronic/carrick/

www.literacyconnections.com/ReadersTheater.html

www. teachingheart.net/readerstheater.htm

www.readerstheatre.ecsd.net/collection.htm

www.fictionteachers.com/classroomtheater/theater.html

www.poetryarchive.org/childrensarchive/home.do

Arnold Lobel or the *Junie B. Jones* books by Barbara Parks provide wonderful opportunities for students to create a script following the text. In addition to the main characters, the texts require a narrator role. In neither case would I expect students to prepare a book-length script; rather, after reading the book, or a part of it, they select one episode to script.

Typically, teachers have overlooked the potential of the popular series books for promoting extensive reading (McGill-Franzen, 1993) and for fostering fluency. Almost all avid readers can recall one or more series of children's books that they literally devoured as they became independent readers. That suggests the power of series books for engaging students in fluency development lessons. Series books make reading easier because they tend to include a standard set of common characters and settings, thereby reducing the number of unique proper nouns that readers have to read. They tend to be written with a common organizational structure and often a common vocabulary. This facilitates both comprehension and repeated exposure to a set of common words. So break out the popular series books for your read-alouds and book displays, and for reader's theater.

For older readers, I am a huge fan of Paul Fleischman's book, *Bull Run* (1995, HarperCollins), as a source of reader's theater activities. The book provides chronological narratives about the horrendous Civil War battle. Several different narrative accounts are provided, ranging from a southern drummer boy and southern civilian to another from a Union soldier. Each narrative is a short telling of the events of the days leading up to and including the battle. I especially like this book because it provides wonderful reader's theater texts as well as rich and curriculum-relevant materials that can provoke powerful discussions. Also on my list of favorites is another book coauthored by Fleischman, *Joyful Noise: Poems for Two Voices* (1988, Harper Trophy).

As for scripts, I prefer the student-scripted variation on reader's theater because it involves a variety of meta-cognitive skills, including locating a specific episode, revising the text into a script, and deciding just how to best dramatize it. But no matter whether you use prepared scripts or student-generated scripts, the goal is a dramatic reenactment, and that will require reading and rereading the script while practicing getting the expression just right. The goal is not memorization of the script, as is the case with acting. As the episode is presented, typically to the whole class, the characters have a copy of the script in their hands, and they read from it.

▶ First-grader Ella loves *Junie B. Jones* books.

As students (even older students) read and reread, they may discover nuances of the character or the episode that they failed to notice on the initial reading (Stayter & Allington, 1991). To produce a dramatic reenactment requires that students think about the context, about the characters' personalities, and about how they might feel and act if they were in the same situation. These sorts of considerations are just what proficient readers do all the time when they read.

A reader's theater event does not have to be a major undertaking; in fact, it should not be. The real value of reader's theater seems to come from the repeated reading of the text and perhaps the discussions about the appropriate expression to be used when delivering the performance.

Reader's theater and other repeated readings techniques produce positive benefits, but the research also shows that, generally, three or four rereadings of a text produce the optimum benefit (Kuhn & Stahl, 2003) and that extensive use of repeated readings techniques is not as effective as combining some repeated readings lessons with the opportunity to engage in extended high-success independent reading (Kuhn, 2005b).

Extended and Deliberate Practice

One reason some beginning readers fail to develop fluent reading is that they simply do not engage in sufficient deliberate, high-success practice (Allington, in press). As Kameenui and Simmons (2001) have argued, the evidence "appears clear and unyielding that practice and exposure to print is essential to fluency" (p. 205).

Although the NRP noted that literally hundreds of studies demonstrated that better readers read much more than weaker readers, the panel also noted that few experimental studies had tested this relationship. In the NRP's view, without experimental studies where the volume of reading was experimentally manipulated, one cannot be sure whether the greater volume of reading caused the better reading or vice-versa. Technically, this is a valid argument, but reading, like every other human proficiency, is surely affected by the amount of practice students engage in.

Today, teachers are given conflicting messages about what research says concerning the effects of reading volume on reading achievement. But the evidence is quite clear that it takes a lot of reading to become a good reader (see Anderson, Wilson, & Fielding, 1988; Cunningham & Stanovich, 1998; Knapp, 1995; Krashen, 2004; Meyer & Wardrop, 1994; National Reading Panel, 2000; Stanovich, 2000; Samuels & Wu, 2003; Stanovich et al., 1996). And the advice to avoid having students read independently during the school day (found in the widely distributed booklet entitled, *Put Reading First*) was not a finding of the NRP and is not supported by the research available. This research includes studies conducted since the NRP report was published (e.g., Lewis & Samuels, 2004), where the impact of including independent reading time was found to be as large as the NRP found for including systematic phonics in reading lesson designs.

However, there is no clear experimental support for answering critical questions such as:

- How much reading volume and what sorts of practice are required to produce fluent oral reading?
- How much guided reading practice (teacher-directed activity) is required?
- How much assigned independent reading practice (student-directed mandated activity) is required?
- How much free voluntary reading (student-directed deliberate activity) should be done?

It is important to consider whether one of these options for enhancing reading volume is more critical in fostering fluent reading than the others. Teachers also need to have better information on each of these options and to know whether there is some optimum ratio of one to the other.

Certainly, reading volume is obviously important, but I think the issue has probably been oversimplified when it comes to developing fluent and proficient readers. It isn't that the simple volume of reading isn't important; it is. But evidence also indicates that teachers need to be more concerned about how much high-success and intrinsically motivated reading students do. A key question that needs to be answered about "independent reading" is whether teacher-assigned and voluntary independent reading have similar or different effects on reading fluency and reading development in general.

I've come to this conclusion after reading widely on the role practice plays in the development of human proficiencies. This research is well summarized in an article by Ericsson, Krampe, and Tesch-Romer (1993). The authors note that practice seems much more related to skill development than an individual's ability. High-level performances in any field are more the result of far greater engagement in practice than in any individual trait. The researchers also conclude that not all practice is equally effective in developing proficiency.

The most powerful form of practice, according to Ericsson and colleagues, is what they term "deliberate practice." This sort of practice is self-motivated, or voluntary. The equivalent for reading development would be what Guthrie (2004) calls "engaged reading" and what Krashen (2004) has labeled free, voluntary reading (FVR). In other words, this powerful form of practice is student-directed, voluntary independent reading.

✭ Free, Voluntary Reading

Many schools exhibit concerns about how much students actually read, but I do not know of any school (or research project) that has focused sustained attention on FVR. Schools or individual teachers may require students to read independently in school each day or at home each night, but the requirement means it is no longer voluntary. So, since reading volume is one critical factor in developing reading fluency, teachers may need to be more concerned about promoting a motivation to read than mandating a certain volume of daily reading.

Free, voluntary reading must be considered if for no other reason than research indicates huge disparities in out-of-school reading volume when more and less proficient readers are compared (Anderson, Wilson, & Fielding, 1988). Some portion of the variance in reading volume may be explained by differences in the reading lessons that more and less proficient readers receive, but it is very difficult to imagine that the tremendous amount of differences reported in the research (e.g., Anderson, Wilson, & Fielding, 1988; Guthrie, 2004) can be wholly explained by what happens during the school day.

So how can you foster greater amounts of FVR both in and out of school? There are four critical features of classrooms designed to increase free, voluntary reading: easy access to interesting books, student choice of what to read, daily teacher read-alouds and other strategies for "blessing books" (Gambrell et al., 1996), and helping put "home-run books" (Trelease, 2001) in every student's hands. I'll address each of these next.

Easy Access to Interesting Books

Two summaries of the research on access (Guthrie & Humenick, 2004; Krashen, 2004) decisively find that improving readers' access to books increases the volume of reading that students do and improves both their motivation for reading and their reading comprehension.

How do schools increase access to interesting books? First and foremost is through supporting the development of classroom library collections of 500 to 800 books (actually titles, because you only count a book once even if there are 25 copies available). The classroom library must reflect the range of reading levels in your classroom so everyone can find interesting books in it. The classroom collections need to be evenly split between informational texts and narratives. Lots of the interesting informational books should be linked to the state science and social studies curriculum topics.

Books in the classroom library should be displayed in interesting and attractive ways, with covers showing as often as possible (Morrow & Weinstein, 1986). This means using rotating wire racks for books rather than traditional bookshelves and smaller targeted displays of thematically linked books on tables or on the top of shelves or filing cabinets.

In addition to large classroom collections that allow fingertip access to interesting books, schools would have open library schedules and helpful library/media specialists. Open library schedules means students can go to the library anytime during the day when they need to find a book to read. In fact, open schedules usually also mean that the library is open before and after school for student library visits (Kaplan, 2007).

Additionally, the school should have a supplemental collection of interesting texts linked to the core curriculum areas (science, social studies, mathematics, health, etc.). These supplemental books should be organized into thematic or topical bins and available for teacher use when needed. In my favorite schools I'll find hundreds of bins of such books organized by grade subject areas and topics and themes. Any teacher can visit the collection and find another 40 or 50 books on the state social studies unit on Native American history in his or her state, for instance. These bins contain books in a range of difficulty levels, so all students will be likely to find several books they can read that supplement any core curriculum material commonly used. If you expect students to become fluent readers, they need high-success reading in science and social studies as well as in reading.

Finally, there is the issue of the level of interest of the texts available. Interest is not just a value of a text but rather is the interaction between the text and the reader's motivation and background knowledge of the text topic(s). In other words, there are books that I might find extremely interesting but that you would find far less so. And the opposite is true as well. You, as a teacher, may select books for your students that you find interesting; that does not mean your students will find those books equally as interesting. In fact, a recent study (Beach, 2006) discovered that there were almost no books that appeared in both the American Library Association's adult-selected *Notable Children's Books* and the International Reading Association's *Children's Choices* (chosen by children). Over the 30-year period this analysis covered (1975–2005), 96 percent of the books appeared on only one of the two lists. Adults and children find very different books interesting.

That said, most classroom book collections are too small and too narrow to fulfill almost anyone's notions of "lots and lots" of interesting texts. This is doubly true for struggling readers in these classrooms. In a study of an effective summer school program (Shin & Krashen, 2008) the researchers noted the barrenness of both the classroom and school libraries and so allocated $25 per student for the purchase of interesting texts. Now this may seem a small amount, but it dramatically improved easy access to interesting books. Imagine if every school allocated this amount every year—there would be no classrooms as barren of interesting books as most are now. One could easily purchase 100 paperbacks per classroom every year. That $25 is far less than most schools already spend on consumable workbooks, duplicating skills sheets, and test preparation materials (Jachym, Allington, & Broikou, 1989)— expenditures that no research supports.

Student Choice

Perhaps this section would be better titled "Creating the Allusion of Choice." I say this because what the research supports is not simply allowing students free choice, per se, but rather *some* choice of what they will be reading. In addition, the research also shows just how powerful teachers can be in creating the motivation to read generally and to read particular books specifically.

What the research demonstrates, in other words, is the impotence of the "everybody reading the same book" model that has so long dominated schools. As in all areas of life, providing individuals with some control over their lives and work produces happier and harder-working people. The same is true with students. Providing some control but allowing a fair amount of personal preference to influence a student's reading diet produces powerful positive effects on engagement and achievement (Guthrie & Humenick, 2004).

In too many classrooms today there are few opportunities for students to exercise choice—one main reason teachers report that motivating students to read is a real problem. But for struggling readers the situation is even more problematic because they have even fewer choices if they want to select a book they can actually read with high success. When given a steady diet of too-hard texts and few opportunities to select what they will read, is it any wonder that so many struggling readers have very limited motivation to read? Designing fluency interventions must include many opportunities for students to choose the books they can and will read if schools are to offer evidence-based interventions.

Daily Read-Alouds and Other Blessings of Books

One way teachers influence students' choices of what books to read is through daily read-alouds. It has been well documented that reading a book aloud increases its appeal and attractiveness for students. But reading aloud seems to be coming less common in classrooms generally and even uncommon in the upper elementary grades as well as in middle school and secondary school classrooms. This is odd because there is a strong research base for the benefits of daily read-alouds that extends well beyond the positive effects of modeling fluent reading (Stahl, 1999).

The teachers who are the most successful at motivating students to read in and out of school are those who constantly "bless" books for students. These blessings are typically brief, less than a minute, but occur all day long, every day of school (Gambrell et al., 1996). Teachers might bless 20 to 30 books every week, or 1,000 or more books every year!

The blessing usually involves simply holding the book up in front of students, mentioning the topic or an attractive characteristic, and perhaps showing an illustration or reading just a very small bit of the book. Oftentimes the blessing also links the content to the work students are doing, have already done, or will be doing in the future. Sometimes teachers mention that a student has read the book and thinks other students will like it. But no matter how the blessing is done, the teacher is constantly hawking new books and exposing the students, ever so briefly, to another possible text they could read.

Home-Run Books

The term *home-run book* comes from Jim Trelease, author of *The Read-Aloud Handbook* (2001). These are books that are simply so engaging for the reader that you may find the student "sneaking a read" when he or she is supposed to be doing something else. These are the books that have the reader saying, "Just let me finish this last bit and then I'll go to recess." Just like a person always remembering his or her first home run, readers remember their first home-run book (for me it was *The Matchlock Gun* by Walter Edmonds).

Many struggling readers have never encountered home-run books. But if you are to succeed in substantially increasing the volume of reading that struggling readers do, and especially increasing the volume of free, voluntary reading they do, you will need to help each struggling reader locate his or her home-run book.

Developmental Differences?

It is unclear to me whether the amount of teacher-directed, assigned independent reading, or free, voluntary reading varies developmentally. Perhaps it seems obvious that at the very initial stages of reading development there would be little free, voluntary reading because at that stage students have developed few of the necessary proficiencies to read independently. But would memory reading of well-rehearsed books be useful practice? What about independent rereading of texts introduced earlier in a shared reading session? Or reading class-made chart stories or one's own writing? Are these potentially intrinsically motivated reading activities important for development?

There are only a handful of studies focused on developmental differences in the most powerful blend of the three types of reading (Connor et al., 2007; Connor, Morrison, & Katch, 2004; McIntyre et al., 2006). However, the evidence from these studies suggests that readers at different developmental levels benefit from different blends of teacher- and student-directed reading activities. In other words, readers need to have developed the ability to read independently and developed the motivation to engage in reading without teacher direction.

Thus, the most effective design of classroom programs targeted for enhancing reading volume as a component of the effort to reduce the number of beginning readers who experience fluency difficulties will likely begin with teacher-directed or teacher-supported activity and then a gradual increase in the amount of student-directed reading across the school year. And in every classroom, efforts to stimulate free, voluntary reading will be ongoing.

☆ Summary

Several aspects of classroom reading lessons can be modified in ways that would more consistently support fluency development, especially lessons for beginning readers.

- By ensuring that the texts used in fluency lessons offer the opportunity for high-success reading activity, teachers can work to foster both greater motivation to read and the acquisition of many words that can be recognized at a glance.

- With appropriate texts there should be many fewer misreadings and thus fewer teacher interruptions of the readers. Adopting something like the pause-prompt-praise strategy should foster expanded self-regulation and greater autonomous strategy use.

- Including more teacher modeling of fluent reading and adding activities such as group choral rereadings or other repeated readings of the texts used in reading lessons provides the sort of support that many readers who struggle with fluency need.

- Ensuring that all students are getting sufficient reading practice (reading volume) must be a concern. This is especially true for the less proficient students who seem also to benefit from increased amounts of teacher-guided reading practice.

- Efforts to foster increased fluency in a greater number of students must also include efforts to stimulate increased amounts of free, voluntary reading, both in and out of school.

- All of these goals will be more easily accomplished if all teachers make easy access to interesting texts and student choice of reading materials common characteristics in all classrooms.

chapter 6

Interventions to Foster Fluency Development in Struggling Readers

Although redesigning the reading lessons typically provided in core reading programs can increase the number of students who avoid problems in developing fluency, it is not clear that such modifications will solve the fluency difficulties of every reader.

Thus, in this chapter I focus primarily on what needs to be done in reading intervention programs to foster fluency in older struggling readers.

When students fail to develop fluent reading skills in the primary grades, they often continue through school as a clunky, word-by-word reader. As Torgeson and Hudson (2006) have noted, research shows that teachers can intervene in ways that develop on-level word reading skills but rarely do these interventions produce fluent readers. These older struggling readers read slowly, if accurately—so slowly that comprehension and reading motivation are impaired.

In an ideal world, all students would receive effective first teaching in the primary grades, and few, if any, would fail to develop into fluent readers by the end of second grade. But until effective first teaching is available in every primary-grade classroom, some readers will struggle with fluency development. This chapter focuses on those readers whose fluency development is off track.

☆ Reconsidering Repeated Readings Interventions

Because the NRP endorsed the repeated readings technique as a "proven" procedure, its use is now far more common in intervention programs than it was a few years ago. Several commercial intervention packages have been constructed with repeated readings as the core activity and these seem to be fairly widely used. I remain concerned, however, that while the repeated readings technique has gained popularity, other research-based intervention techniques are being overlooked, and the limitations of the repeated readings technique are going unrecognized.

It now seems clear that the major reason for the success of repeated readings as an intervention strategy is that it expands reading volume when implemented. In other words, time spent engaged in repeatedly reading texts replaces time that was previously spent on other activities such as skills worksheets. Kuhn's research (2005a, 2007) provides a clear demonstration of the positive effects of replacing much repeated readings activity with extended opportunities for independent reading. So, while some of the limitations of the technique have been made more visible, there remains, I believe, a potentially powerful role for repeated readings to play in interventions designed to promote fluency development.

For older readers who seem to habitually read word-by-word, even when reading accuracy is high, the repeated readings technique seems an appropriate initial intervention. By initial intervention, I mean that a few weeks of use of the repeated readings technique seems a powerful strategy for allowing those word-by-word readers to get themselves unstuck from print and reading in phrases with expression. But after a few weeks, the intervention design needs to initiate greater amounts of independent reading while reducing the amount of time spent in repeatedly reading texts. The time allocations might look something like those illustrated in Table 6.1.

After nine weeks of intervention using the repeated readings technique the teacher would transition the readers into extended independent reading activity and largely eliminate repeated readings. Of course, she or he might still plan for lessons that required students to read a text several times, using a reader's theater activity, for instance. But since few studies of the repeated readings extended to even nine weeks in length, there is little research support for the long-term use of repeated readings in an intervention design.

There are also some pretty consistent findings in the research about the key elements of an effective repeated readings lesson design. Therrien (2003) conducted a meta-analysis on 18 repeated readings intervention studies and reported that the following features were associated with greater gains:

- Before beginning a repeated readings activity, cue the children to focus on both fluency and comprehension.

- Set a target reading rate (wcpm) rather than require a set number of rereadings.

▶ Table 6.1   **Changing time allocations in a fluency intervention**

	Repeated readings	Independent reading
Weeks 1–3	90%	10%
Weeks 4–6	50%	50%
Weeks 7–9	10%	90%

- Whenever possible, have an adult, preferably a teacher, model and monitor the repeated readings (rather than using audiotapes or peer tutors).
- Use texts matched to student reading levels, not grade-level texts.
- Chart or graph student performances (or have the students do this).

The largest gains in fluency seem to appear first on the texts that have been repeatedly read, but typically there is no transfer of fluency when reading new texts. But with more and more experience, the transfer of reading in phrases with expression to new texts is observed. All this can and should happen after no more than 6 to 9 weeks' use of the repeated readings technique. Such progress also assumes that the teacher is measuring reading rate, accuracy, and fluency on independent-level texts, not grade-level texts. Remember, the first step in turning a struggling reader into an achieving reader is to make that student a good reader at his or her current reading level. Once that fourth-grade struggling reader reads like a good second-grade reader, then you can worry about increasing his or her reading level.

Designing Individual Repeated Readings Lessons

The first step to designing individual repeated readings lessons is to select students who would seem to benefit from lessons focused on fluency. This may seem obvious, but too often interventions take on a one-size-fits-all approach rather than being tailored to meet the needs of the struggling readers being served (Buly & Valencia, 2002; McGill-Franzen & Allington, 1990; Vaughn, Moody, & Schumm, 1998). The ideal candidates for repeated reading lessons are those struggling readers who read largely word-by-word (Level 1 or 2 on the fluency scale) even when given passages that they read with good accuracy.

The next step is selecting texts appropriate for the repeated readings activity. By and large, these texts need to be at the student's independent reading level, read with 99 percent accuracy. Typically, this will mean you will have to look beyond the texts found in the core reading program. An ideal text would have few rare or infrequent words and few proper nouns.

The third step is selecting an appropriate target wcpm for the student. This can be tricky, so I suggest you use a combination of the wcpm grade level norms found on page 64 and the student's initial wcpm calculated on the first reading of the passage. Remember that the appropriate grade level for selecting norms is the student's reading level, not his or her grade-placement level. But, at least initially, even the reading-level wcpm norms may be a challenge. So, if on the initial reading of the passage the student produces a wcpm substantially below reading-level norms, set the standard below the reading level but 10 to 20 wcpm above the level obtained on the initial reading. After a few weeks the reading-level wcpm norms should become the appropriate target standard.

Now you have the student (or students) selected, the text selected, and the standard selected. It is time to begin the lesson. To open the *initial lessons* using the repeated readings technique, I suggest you use an adaptation of the assisted reading model. As Smith's (1979) study demonstrated, the use of teacher modeling by reading the text aloud to students produces earlier success than having the students do the initial reading themselves. In fact, for the first lessons you may simply want to have the readers read along with you on each reading and rereading. This seems especially useful for older students who seem wholly unable to read fluently and have had years of word-by-word reading experience.

Regardless of how you structure the repeated readings activity, you should consider introducing any words you know will pose problems for the reader before having the student read a text solo. If you find that there are lots of such words, you need to consider whether the text you've selected is appropriate for fluency development. Of course, this step is less important if you continue to use the assisted reading model and read along with the students, but even then it may be useful to isolate some words and provide a quick lesson on why these words are pronounced the way they are and what they mean.

Following the guidelines from the research before any reading or rereading, focus attention on both fluency and comprehension. As the student rereads the text, continue to focus on both. The comprehension focus should not, however, become an activity that simply emphasizes the literal recall of details from the text. Instead, ask the reader to summarize, to question motives or actions, to link the text to his or her own experiences, and so on.

As the student begins his or her first attempt at reading the text without your support, remember to record the time it took to complete the reading. This is most easily accomplished if you have an inexpensive timer or stopwatch that allows you to record the time spent reading. While the reader is reading, you also need to track the accuracy of his or her reading. As noted in

Chapter 4, there are several well-established procedures for recording reading performance, and it matters little which method you use. Likewise, you need to monitor the fluency of the reading following the NAEP four-point fluency rating scale (see page 71).

You will need to decide how you will respond if the student encounters a word he or she simply cannot pronounce even after repeated attempts. My own approach is to provide the word if, after several attempts, the student seems frustrated and unwilling to continue. I don't interrupt just because the student misreads a word, although I would return to that word after the reading is completed and ask the student to then reread the sentence the word appears in. At that point I would initially ask whether the misread makes sense. If it does but still is not the correct word, I'd ask the student to look at the word and ask, "Can that word be XXXX? Let's look at all the letters." Now, if the misread word is not readily decodable—remember the example of "tongue"—I would likely pronounce the word correctly and say something similar to, "I know the word looks like /tahn-goo/, but it is pronounced *tongue*. Reread the sentence, and see how it sounds now."

The real goal when working on misread words is to support the reader in using the skills he or she has available to figure out the word without help. You also want to foster increased self-monitoring by the reader. Jumping in and simply supplying the word may undermine both of these goals (Allington, 1980; McGill-Franzen & McDermott, 1978).

After the student has completed each reading and rereading, help the student chart his or her rate, accuracy, and fluency performances. Reproducible forms for these purposes are located in Appendix A. This recording makes progress visible to the student and to you. Take care, though, that this charting event is done efficiently so as to not occupy very much instructional time (see Figure 6.1).

Designing Small-Group Repeated Readings Lessons

When working with a small group of struggling readers, the basic lesson plan is the same, but when selecting texts to be read, you must consider the range of individual differences among the readers in the group. You need to select texts that allow each reader to be successful. If the achievement levels vary

► Figure 6.1   **Repeated readings graph (shows increasing reading rate and decreasing uncorrected word reading errors)**

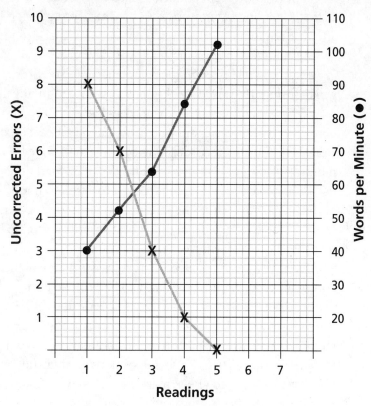

Source: Adapted from S. A. Stahl (2003).

substantially among members of the group, this will not be easy and may indicate that you need to select two or more texts and create even smaller groups.

Repeated Readings Lessons without Adult Support

Although research has demonstrated that teacher support and involvement in the repeated readings activity produces better results than when students work alone, there are times when teacher support is not feasible. In those cases researchers have found that lessons can be adapted and still produce benefits for struggling readers.

One method, Tape-Check-Chart, uses an audiotape recorder in support of fluent reading (Allington, 2006b). This lesson design is probably best used after the students have completed several teacher-guided repeated readings lessons and have become familiar with the process.

First, you will need to locate an audiotape recorder for each student who will be using the Tape-Check-Chart lesson design. Ideally, the tape recorder would have a counter that advances as the tape recording is being made. Even better, you will find headphones and maybe even a voice microphone that work with the tape recorder. The counter makes it easy for the reader to monitor reading rate and eliminates the need for a timer. The headphones are useful because they allow the student to listen to her or his reading without bothering anyone else. The microphone is useful because the reader doesn't have to read as loudly to make a good audio-recording. Even a basic tape recorder, however, will work fine.

Once you have selected the text the student will read and located an audiotape recorder, you are ready to begin. The basic procedure is for the student to read the text and tape-record his or her reading. When done reading, the student records the counter number and then rewinds the tape. Next, the student listens to his or her reading and marks each word he or she misread. For this marking I use a four-color ink pen. After the first reading, I have the student put a red check mark over each word misread. Then the tape is rewound to the beginning, and the student rereads the text while recording his or her reading. Again, the student records the counter number, rewinds the tape, and listens to his or her reading, putting a green check mark above each word misread. Finally, the student completes a third rereading and puts a blue check mark above each word misread.

Now the student is ready to chart his or her performances. The student can chart the rate by charting the numbers from the counter on the tape recorder. To chart accuracy, he or she needs to count the red, green, and blue check marks on the text and chart each one. Improvement is observed when the number on the counter and the number of errors get smaller after each reading. You can find a reproducible form in Appendix A where accuracy and rate can both be charted for each text read.

Both of these approaches to designing repeated readings lessons have been demonstrated to have positive effects on fluency and accuracy, especially on the texts the readers are rereading. Both are good short-term intervention strategies. It seems useful to begin the initial fluency lessons with teacher support and only then move to the Tape-Check-Chart option. Although the repeated readings technique has been shown effective in improving fluency on the practice texts, there is less evidence of transfer to new texts than might be expected.

Thus, my recommendation is that repeated readings be used as a short-term intervention strategy to help older struggling readers begin to understand what fluent reading is all about. If you want older struggling readers to become fluent, expressive readers, then focus on their volume of reading.

Reading Volume and the Struggling Reader

Regarding closing the reading fluency gap among older struggling readers, Torgeson and Hudson (2006) of the Florida Center for Reading Research state:

> The most important factor appears to involve difficulties in making up for the huge deficits in accurate reading practice the older children have accumulated by the time they reach later elementary school. . . . One of the major results of this lack of reading practice is a severe limitation in the number of words the children with reading disabilities can recognize automatically, or at a single glance. . . . Such "catching up" would seem to require an extensive period of time in which the reading practice of the previously disabled children was actually greater than that of their peers. Even if word reading accuracy is dramatically increased through more efficient use of analytical word-reading processes, reliance on analytic processes will not produce the kind of fluent reading that results when most words in a passage can be recognized at a single glance. (pp. 147–148)

In other words, older struggling readers probably will never become fluent and proficient readers unless teachers design interventions that dramatically increase the volume of reading that they do (Allington, 1977, 2006b).

Guthrie (2004) reviewed the research on reading volume and concluded that "because engaged readers spend 500 percent more time reading than disengaged students, educators should attempt to increase engaged reading time by 200–500 percent" (p. 1). He also noted that accomplishing this will likely require a considerable reorganizing of the current curriculum and current classroom and intervention designs. In other words, these leading researchers concluded that current school responses to struggling readers miss the big point—volume of reading matters critically in the development of fluent, proficient readers.

Techniques such as repeated readings can help older struggling readers read well-practiced texts fluently, but it takes a different intervention model to turn older struggling readers into typically fluent readers. Central to the design of any intervention for older struggling readers has to be the monitoring and expanding of struggling readers' volume of reading. When the reading

One potentially powerful strategy for fluency development is pairing older struggling readers with younger developing readers. In these cases the older struggling readers read and reread a book appropriate for reading aloud to the younger students. Every week the older students travel to meet the younger students. Once there, the older students read the books and then engage the younger students in discussions about the books.

Several versions of this arrangement have been used, including sessions where older struggling students work with and read to younger struggling readers during the session. This sort of session requires that the older struggling readers have been coached on working with younger struggling readers. In the photo you can see such a partnership actually working.

▶ This middle school student is reading to a first-grader to develop fluency.

volume of struggling readers lags well behind that of other students for several years, they accumulate enormous deficits. By fourth grade, for instance, struggling readers have read millions fewer words than their achieving classmates. They have read for hundreds of hours less than those classmates. Some of these differences can be accounted for by the difference in the amount of reading struggling readers are asked to do in school. But most of the difference in reading volume is accounted for by variations in the time spent in free, voluntary reading by struggling and achieving readers.

Quite honestly, it seems unlikely that educators will be very successful in convincing most struggling older readers to engage in lots of voluntary reading because they have learned to dislike reading. Thus, any intervention for older struggling readers needs a two-pronged approach.

The first prong is teacher-directed reading lessons that include substantial amounts of reading activity. These older struggling readers need both useful and explicit instruction in developing many important skills and strategies, along with lots of teacher-guided reading. Most intervention designs have generally emphasized the former but not the latter.

Evidence shows how important emphasizing actual reading in the intervention design can be (Allington et al., 2007; Scanlon et al., 2005; Vadasy, Sanders, & Peyton, 2005). Distinguished learning disabilities researcher Frank Vellutino (2003) has detailed the many advantages of wide reading as a central component in intervention design:

> One way to develop linguistic competencies is through extensive and diverse reading, because it is largely through reading that one encounters the more complex, the more abstract, and the more varied forms of language. Extensive and diverse reading is also the primary means by which children acquire discourse knowledge, that is, knowledge about the structural characteristics of different text types (e.g., narrative and informational) that is so important for interpreting and organizing the text. Extensive and diverse reading is also an important way to acquire world knowledge and domain specific knowledge and to increase reading fluency and proficiency. (pp. 74–75)

Thus, I suggest that 70 percent of the intervention period be allocated to reading activity, including both teacher-guided and student-directed independent reading. The remaining time would be spent on skill and strategy instruction useful for fostering the development in each struggling reader.

The second prong is a focus on fostering free, voluntary reading outside the intervention period. As Vellutino (2003) has argued, "Obviously, instruction that capitalizes on children's inherent interests and surrounds them with high-interest reading materials at their level of proficiency is more effective than instruction that does less" (p. 77). Thus, Fink's interest-based reading intervention (Fink, 2006), designed from her studies of successful adult dyslexic readers, seems a good fit, although the very successful Benchmark School model shares many similar characteristics (Gaskins, 2005).

The central issue here is crafting an intervention that helps struggling readers locate texts they can read and want to read. Thus, it is unlikely that any commercial intervention package will be of any help. Central to almost all commercial intervention packages is the small supply of standard texts that every student works through. That isn't interest-based design; it is profit-center design.

There are a few commercial products that do provide a substantial array of texts for students to choose from, such as *Accelerated Reader* (Renaissance Learning), *Read 180,* and *Reading Counts* (both from Scholastic). But the research on these products is mixed, with even the better studies showing only small effects on achievement, and the number of published studies is small (Hasselbring & Goin, 2004; Krashen, 2003; Nunnery, Ross, & McDonald, 2006). In addition, as Guthrie (2004) noted, struggling readers need more than just the independent practice these programs can provide. They also need a great deal of teacher-guided reading lessons.

Two Powerful Resources for Interest-Based Interventions

Fink, R. (2006). *Why Jane and Johnny Couldn't Read—And How They Learned.* Newark, DE: International Reading Association.

Gaskins, I. W. (2005). *Success with Struggling Readers: The Benchmark School Approach.* New York: Guilford.

I have other concerns about packaged products. Experts know, for instance, that use of these products in elementary schools does not produce greater amounts of free, voluntary reading in older students (Pavonetti, Brimmer, & Cipielewski, 2003). In other words, use of these products does not seem to foster longer-term reading habits. The packages provide many more narrative books than informational books and include small numbers of culturally relevant books for minority students (Lamme, Fu, & Allington, 2002). Finally, although the packages do provide a school with a large supply of children's books and, typically, a method for helping teachers and students locate books that are of an appropriate level of difficulty, all of this is usually very mechanical, often unreliable, and typically more expensive than are books purchased outside of the package.

A recent large-scale experimental study supported by the U.S. Department of Education could find no improvement in reading achievement when schools used technology-based commercial packages like these. I am not surprised, because it is teachers who know their students best—both their interests and their reading levels. I just cannot imagine any computer software being better able than an effective teacher at helping a struggling reader find a book he or she can read—a book he or she can't wait to begin.

As the Guthrie and Humenick (2004) meta-analysis demonstrated, creating schools where struggling readers have easy access to interesting and appropriate books all day long must become a central theme in designing interventions for struggling readers. Likewise, allowing struggling readers to select many, if not most, of the texts they will read is also a critical design factor.

Getting older struggling readers to read independently is typically not a problem once they have easy access to interesting and appropriate books and magazines. But how long should you expect struggling readers to read each day? Samuels and Wu (2003) found that adding as little as 15 minutes of daily independent reading improved the reading achievement of struggling readers. Many poor readers, however, seemed to have difficulty reading independently for more than 15 minutes, perhaps because they had so little voluntary reading experience. It might be that, at least initially, teachers would need to schedule several 15-minute periods each day for struggling readers to read independently. Teachers might also need to check in with struggling readers after 15 minutes of independent reading and engage them in brief discussions of what they have read, asking for summaries, predictions, and problems they are having. With greater experience with independent reading, struggling readers may develop the stamina to read for longer periods of time.

One way to benchmark the appropriate volume of reading would be to monitor the volume of reading that on-level readers are doing in and out of school. Fielding, Wilson, and Anderson (1986) used activity logs to monitor how fifth-grade students spent their time outside of school. On average, these students spent about 15 to 20 minutes reading at home each day, not counting homework-related reading. About half of this time was spent reading books and the remainder reading comics, magazines, newspapers, and so on. But the lowest-achieving students rarely read books and did little reading of any type. The best readers read a lot, more than an hour a day of free, voluntary book reading.

If students read for 20 minutes a day outside school, that produces 1 to 1.5 million words read each year (using 150- and 200-word per minute silent reading rates). Those struggling readers who read nothing outside school are becoming less and less likely to ever become proficient readers. But if educators could design interventions that resulted in struggling readers voluntarily reading 20 to 30 minutes each day over and above the reading the typical students are doing, teachers would be on course to allow the struggling readers to slowly catch up to the better readers.

If teachers could create interventions that helped struggling readers find books and magazines and other materials they could read and really want to read, teachers might even get them excited about reading voluntarily outside of school. This would work to close the volume gap even more quickly. Stanovich and colleagues (1996) noted, "Free-reading choices may explain part of the puzzle and the pressing social problem of widening disparities between the educational haves and have nots" (p. 28).

Reading volume is a critical though often neglected feature of a research-based intervention to develop fluent reading in older struggling readers. Implementing the research-based guidelines for helping struggling readers achieve the necessary reading volume will require many schools to dramatically alter both their planning and purchases. It isn't that there is too little funding to create the sorts of schools that will provide easy access to an abundance of interesting and appropriate texts, it is the understanding of what the research says that seems to be lacking.

At-a-Glance Words

Recall that one reason that reading volume is so critical in developing fluency is the role that extensive high-success reading plays in building a reader's store of at-a-glance words. There are two design features involved here. First is planning to dramatically increase the volume of reading that struggling readers do each and every day. Second, the benefits of wide reading are most powerful when the reading is high-accuracy, high-success reading (99% accuracy). This is because for any word to become an at-a-glance word, the reader has to read it correctly multiple times.

To ensure that word recognition for story words is well developed, teachers might elect to focus on some of the words that seem likely to present decoding difficulties for some or all the students involved in the lesson. Typically, this focus would come after the initial reading aloud of the story to the students.

To focus on particular words would involve isolating those words, perhaps writing them on the blackboard or on a wall chart. The teacher then would discuss with students the "whys" of each word's pronunciation. This could involve comparing and contrasting (Cunningham, 2004) the new word with other known words (demonstrating the "use what you know to figure out what you don't know" strategy). For instance, in one core reading program, the story *Beatrice Doesn't Want To* is an excerpt from the book of the same name by Laura Joffe Numeroff. I might select words such as *report, brand, shelf, stuck, soaking,* and *poster* to focus on after the first shared reading.

I would write those words on chart paper and then proceed through each word, noticing why the word is pronounced the way it is. For *report*, I'd break it into *re/port* and probably then also write *fort* and *sort* on the chart and notice that these words rhyme with and are spelled the same as the final part of *report*. For *brand*, I'd notice the *and* as well as the *br* that is also found in *brown* and *bring*. For *shelf*, I'd notice the *elf*, and so on. I'd hope to be able to do this activity in 2 to 3 minutes. The activity is designed simply to give readers the opportunity to "notice" why a word is pronounced the way it is as well as a modeling of the "use what you know" strategy.

I would leave the chart in a place where it was available for review by the students or perhaps put these six words on a class word wall where they would be available for review. Alternatively, and especially if a big book version of the text is available, I could simply have the student "box" the words with their fingers in their books and quickly note the whys of pronunciation.

This small excursion into word teaching cannot become a major component of the lesson, however. If there are too many words that the students are likely to have difficulty with, then it is time to reconsider use of the classroom core reading program materials, at least for fostering fluency.

Nonetheless, a focus on word pronunciation is not a bad thing, to say the least. If the struggling reader(s) I was working with still had difficulty with many of the high-frequency words (see Appendix B for the Dolch 220 Word list), then I would design a daily 5- to 10-minute lesson component that focused on developing the accurate and rapid identification of these words. There have been mixed results in the research for training the recognition of these words in isolation (Dahl & Samuels, 1977; Nicholson & Tan, 1999). I think the problem is that neither feature—work in isolation nor work in context—is necessarily sufficient.

For work in isolation the critical factor is getting the struggling reader to attend to the internal structure of the word—that is, the order of the letters. One strategy that I have found effective in accomplishing this is the Word Wall Spelling Test (Cunningham & Allington, 2007). Word walls have become a common feature in many primary-grade classrooms because of the demonstrated potential for helping beginning readers learn to read the high-frequency but often not very decodable words.

To create a word wall, you select the high-frequency words (use the Dolch Word list for this) that appear in the texts the students will be reading. You might focus only on the high-frequency words you know the reader(s) have difficulty with. Write those words with a thick marker on card stock, usually 3" × 5" cards work fine. Post the focus cards on the wall.

For the Word Wall Spelling Test, you simply read the words from the wall, use them in a sentence, and then have the students write the words as in the typical spelling test. But what isn't typical is that the students can look at the word wall as they spell the words. After some practice you could face them away from the word wall and let them turn around and look only when they are sure they are unsure about how to spell the word.

This activity forces students to write the high-frequency words and in doing so to pay attention to the sequence of letters in each word. If you leave the word wall posted and add new words over time, the task becomes harder but students also can use it in editing their writing (or ensuring they spell the

Some English words are used very frequently. For instance, only 100 words make up roughly half of all the words you will ever read in texts. These are words such as *a, the, is, was, and, of, be, for,* and *to.* There are a number of compilations of the most frequent words but the grandfather of all high-frequency word lists is the Dolch 220 (Dolch, 1936). The words on the Dolch list and the other more recent lists largely overlap. Because the Dolch 220 excludes nouns, the other lists differ slightly. You can find the Dolch 220 most frequent word list in Appendix B and at the websites listed here. The websites also include ideas for teaching these high-frequency words.

http://literacyconnections.com/Dolch1.html

www.janbrett.com/games/jan_brett_dolch_word_list_main.htm

www.mrsperkins.com/dolch.htm

high-frequency words correctly as they write). Too often teachers seem to forget the powerful link between spelling and word recognition and, because of this, fail to take advantage of the power of writing to help students acquire accurate word recognition skills. Using a word wall as a writing support or as an editing tool is a powerful but simple strategy for taking advantage of the reading/writing relationship (Cunningham, 2004).

One other student-directed activity that can be used as a center activity is modeled after the game "Concentration." You create two cards for each word, perhaps 3" × 5" index cards. You shuffle the deck of these cards, usually 20 or so, and then lay them face down on a table. One student can compete against himself or herself, or two or three students can compete with each other in turning cards over one at a time and then turning over a second card to see if it is the matching card. If it is, the student keeps the matching cards. If not, both cards are returned, face down, to the table and the next player tries to find two cards that match. This game involves visually remembering the words. A variation requires the student to read the word correctly as each card is picked up. I find this variation works best when you or another adult are present just to ensure the word card is read correctly.

Three Strikes and You're Out

One strategy for focusing on at-a-glance vocabulary development is the Three Strikes and You're Out activity. The student, with your help, selects words to learn from the materials he or she is currently reading. Remember that only a few words should be selected each week (5 to 10 words) and that those words should be rather high-frequency words with which the reader has exhibited some difficulty in reading.

Have the student make a card for each word. You may need to model an appropriate font size and neatness for some kids. Once the words have been written on the cards, play a flashcard word reading game. On the initial trials through the words, give the reader 2 to 3 seconds to see each word and then cover the word. If the word is read incorrectly or not read, put the cards in the "no" pile. When the word is read correctly, put it in the "yes" pile and place a check on the back of the card.

After you have gone through all of the words, return to the "no" cards and give the reader as long as she or he needs before requiring the child to say the word. When necessary, teach word parts or cue the use of decoding tools to figure out the word. If the reader doesn't pronounce the word correctly, tell him or her the word and have the student repeat the word, spell the word, and name it again.

When the word cards have three checks on the reverse, they can be removed from the training pile. Remember the three checks must be three *consecutive* correct readings. They now go into the at-a-glance pile, where the reader has to pronounce the word immediately right after a very brief exposure of the word card. Each correct pronunciation gets an X written on the back of the card. Three consecutive Xs and the card is removed from the assessment activity.

★ Summary

In designing research-based interventions to foster fluency development in older struggling readers, you must remember the substantial—maybe *enormous* is a better word—reading practice deficit these readers have

At the end of each week, record on the graph available in Appendix A the total number or words the reader had read correctly three consecutive times after a brief exposure to the word. In graphing you simply add the new words each week to the total number of words the reader has accumulated so far.

"Three Strikes and You're Out." This student exceeded the goal of learning 100 words in 14 weeks. He did it in 12 weeks.

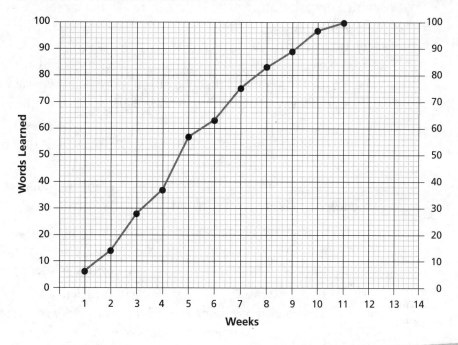

accumulated. The best evidence available suggests that this millions-of-words deficit in high-success reading volume is at the root of their difficulties.

Although the NRP endorsed the repeated readings technique for fostering fluency in struggling readers, I am less optimistic about the longer-term use of this instructional strategy. The repeated readings technique seems to work in the research because using the technique typically increases the volume of reading that the struggling readers do. It also provides multiple successful exposures to the words in the text being read and reread. But most research on the repeated readings technique demonstrated larger improvements on the texts being read and reread than on other texts. Most of the repeated readings interventions lasted 10 weeks or less and thus there is little support for using this strategy as a single, long-term intervention.

However, the research is clear that expanding the reading volume of struggling readers is an essential feature of successful interventions designs. I've argued that what struggling readers seem to need most is greater amounts of purposeful, voluntary reading along with increased teacher-directed reading activity.

Given the evidence available and my best professional advice from clinical experiences, I recommend the following if more than a very few pupils in your classroom are reading dysfluently (word-by-word with little expression).

1. Ensure that these pupils are practicing every day in texts they can actually read with a high-level of accuracy (98 percent or better).

2. Foster adoption of the "pause-prompt-praise" interaction pattern whenever pupils are reading aloud.

3. Consider using one of the repeated readings techniques that involves reading with/to a fluent model (e.g., choral reading, reading with audiotape support, echo reading) for one or two days a week for a few weeks.

4. Ask whether these students are engaging in sufficient amounts of high-success free, voluntary reading every day. If not, consider what needs to be changed to produce greater amounts of FVR.

Afterword

You might be disappointed that nowhere in this book have I endorsed any of the several commercially available products marketed as useful in developing reading fluency. My lack of endorsement should not be read as condemnation of all commercial products. I am not basically "anti-materials" but I am, at the heart, a true believer in the power of expert teachers to solve almost any instructional problem or learning difficulty.

We do not need any more studies of the critical nature of expert teachers when it comes to developing reading proficiencies in the classroom or clinic (Nye, Konstantopoulos, & Hedges, 2004; Pressley et al., 2001). Unfortunately, U.S. schools typically do not have nearly as many expert reading teachers as they need. As a result, in too many schools paraprofessionals provide much of the instruction for struggling readers in federally funded remedial reading and resource room programs for pupils with learning disabilities. The hope, it seems, is that by purchasing some slick, packaged commercial reading program for classroom or intervention lessons, inexpert adults will somehow come to solve the reading problems of struggling readers. But we have 60 years of evidence that this approach has not worked. At the same time, we have 60 years of research on the critical nature of teacher expertise—research that continues to be largely ignored.

So why hasn't federal and state educational policy followed the research findings on the importance of expertise? My view is that until the No Child Left Behind Act came along, no one in schools actually worried very much about whether struggling readers became proficient readers. They simply took the extra funding and spent it on something, even if that something hadn't actually worked in the previous decade or two. With the NCLB focus on adequate yearly progress and with its penalties for failing to design interventions that solve the problems of struggling readers, schools are suddenly focused on the progress, or lack of it, being made by struggling readers.

This is all good in my view, but a very real problem with NCLB is that it again privileges commercial reading packages over teacher expertise. And in too many schools, it isn't just that the commercial product is privileged but that "just follow the program guide" mandates are usurping the autonomy that expert teachers need in order to adapt and modify reading lessons to best fit the readers in front of them. No packaged program can truly be considered research-based if only because we have a century's worth of research demonstrating the absolutely critical nature of fitting instruction to the child you are trying to teach. And since children differ in so many ways, it is literally impossible to craft a single standard lesson that will best fit the needs of each student in the nation's diverse schools and communities.

It may be that using a commercial program produces a better result than doing nothing (the usual comparison made in "scientific" studies) and it may even do a bit better when compared to weak or poorly designed instruction. But packaged programs do not produce better results; expert teachers do. It is when expert teachers select a commercial product based on the unique needs of the student they are working with, and then adapt that product in ways that serves the needs of the student, that commercial packages might produce good outcomes.

In closing this book, I will simply ask: Does your school have an adequate supply of expert teachers of reading? If your response is, "No, we don't," then we know where the problem lies, and it isn't with the students having difficulty acquiring fluency or reading proficiently.

> You can find out about what scientific research is available and what that research says about 20 reading programs at **www.whatworks.ed.gov**. You can also see the list of over 100 reading programs that no scientific research supports. While the folks at the What Works Clearinghouse have not created a perfect document in this review of reading materials, it is the closest thing yet to something like the Consumers Guide for reading programs.

Appendix A

Reproducibles

Weekly Oral Reading wcpm Data
over a 12-Week Intervention

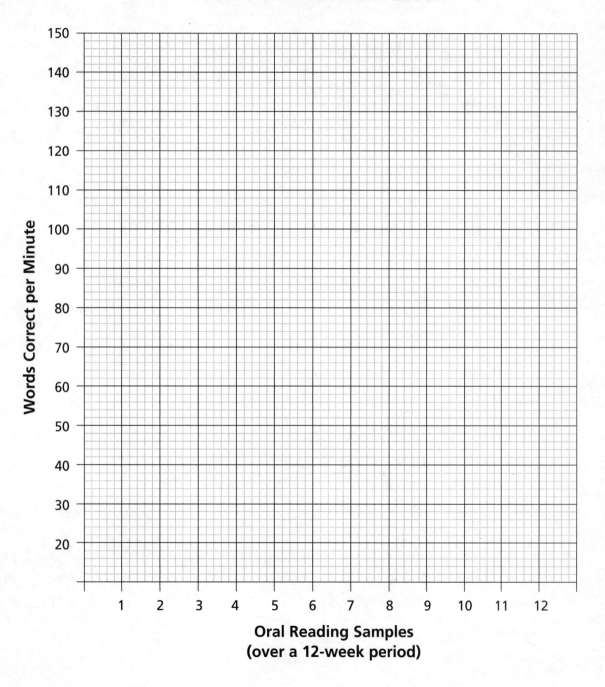

Fluency Graphing

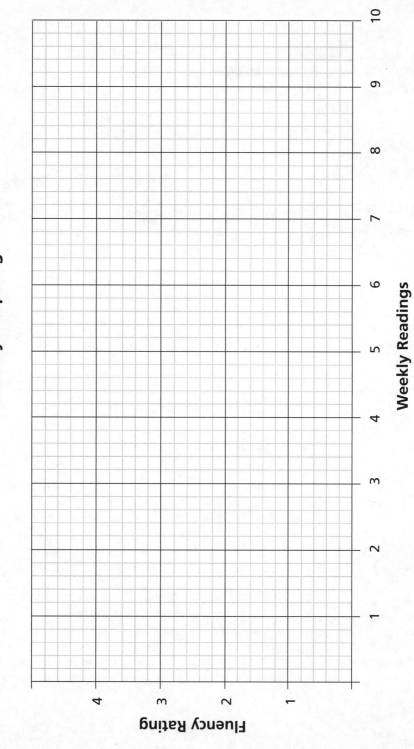

Fluency Rating

Weekly Readings

Repeated Readings Graph

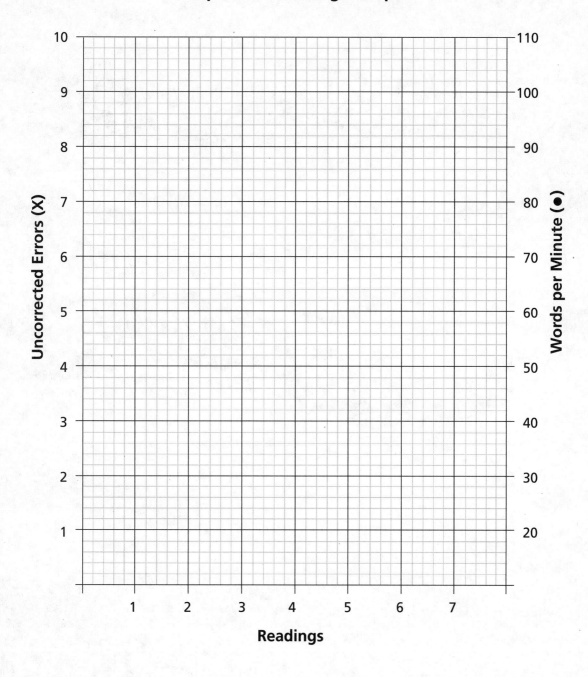

Uncorrected Errors (X)

Words per Minute (●)

Readings

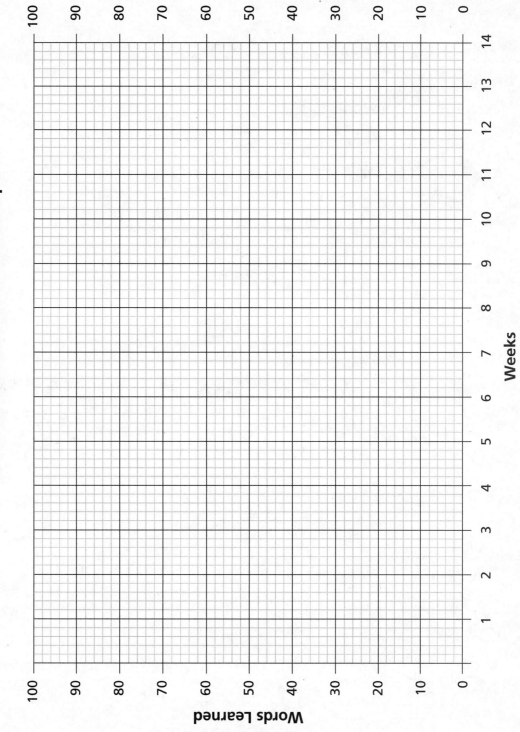

Three Strikes and You're Out Graph

Words Learned

Weeks

Appendix B

Dolch Sight Word List

Preprimer	Primer	First	Second	Third
a	all	after	always	about
and	am	again	around	better
away	are	an	because	bring
big	at	any	been	carry
blue	ate	as	before	clean
can	be	ask	best	cut
come	black	by	both	done
down	brown	could	buy	draw
find	but	every	call	drink
for	came	fly	cold	eight
funny	did	from	does	fall
go	do	give	don't	far
help	eat	going	fast	full
hers	four	had	first	got
I	get	has	five	grow
in	good	her	found	hold
is	has	him	gave	hot
it	he	how	goes	hurt
jump	into	just	green	if
little	like	know	its	keep

Source: http://gemini.es.brevard.K12.fl.us/sheppard/reading/dolch.html.

Preprimer	Primer	First	Second	Third
look	must	let	made	kind
make	new	live	many	laugh
me	no	may	off	light
my	now	of	or	long
not	on	old	pull	much
one	our	once	read	myself
play	out	open	right	never
red	please	over	sing	only
run	pretty	put	sit	own
said	ran	round	sleep	pick
see	ride	some	tell	seven
the	saw	stop	their	shall
three	say	take	these	show
to	she	thank	those	six
two	so	them	upon	small
up	soon	then	us	start
we	that	think	use	ten
yellow	there	walk	very	today
you	they	where	wash	together
	this	when	which	try
	too		why	warm
	under		wish	
	want		work	
	was		would	
	well		write	
	went		your	
	what			
	white			
	who			
	will			
	with			
	yes			

Book Study Guide
for
What Really Matters in Fluency

prepared by Lisa Wiedmann

Book Study Guidelines

Reading, reacting, and interacting with others about a book is one of the ways many of us process new information. Book studies are a common feature in many school districts because they recognize the power of collaborative learning. The intent of a book study is to provide a supportive context for accessing new ideas and affirming best practices already in place. Marching through the questions in a lockstep fashion could result in the mechanical processing of information; it is more beneficial to select specific questions to focus on and give them the attention they deserve.

One possibility to structure your book discussion of *What Really Matters in Fluency* is to use the Reading Reaction Sheet on page 130. Following this format, make a copy for each group member. Next, select a different facilitator for each chapter. The facilitator will act as the official note taker and be responsible for moving the discussion along. He or she begins by explaining that the first question is provided to start the group discussion. The remaining three questions are to be generated by the group. The facilitator can ask each person to identify at least one question and then let the group choose the three they want to cover, or the facilitator can put the participants into three groups, with each group responsible for identifying one question. The three questions are shared for all to hear (and write down), and then discussion of Question 1 commences. The facilitator paces the discussion so the most relevant information for that group is brought out. Since many school districts require documentation for book studies, the facilitator could file the sheet with the appropriate person as well as distribute a copy to all group members for their notes.

Another possibility is to use the guiding questions for each chapter. You could have the same facilitator for all chapters. Perhaps this would be someone who read the book first and suggested it to the group. Or the facilitator role could rotate. It is suggested that the facilitator not only pace the group through the questions to hit on the most important information for the group's needs, but he or she should take notes for later distribution to group members and/or administrators if required for documentation.

The provided questions are meant to provoke discussion and might lead the group into areas not addressed in the questions. That is wonderful! The importance of a book study is to move the members along in their understanding of the book content. If time is limited, the facilitator might select certain questions from the list for the initial focus of the discussion, allowing other questions as time permits.

Of course, a third option is to combine the two structures. Select the format that best fits your group and the time frame you have set for completion of the book.

All book sessions should end with a purpose for reading the next chapter. It could be to generate questions the group still has, to find implications for each person's own teaching, or to identify new ideas. Purpose setting is a time-honored way to help readers (of any age) approach the text. If you are using the questions that accompany each chapter, direct the participants to read the questions prior to reading the chapter. This will provide a framework for processing the information in the chapter.

Book Study Questions for Each Chapter

chapter 1: What Is Fluency and Why Is It "Hot"?

1. What strategies from this chapter do you see yourself using? Why?
2. Generate a question this chapter caused you to wonder about. Bring it to the group for discussion.
3. Allington presents three definitions of *fluency*. Thinking in terms of strongly agree, agree, or disagree, look at each definition and determine which one you feel is most accurate.
4. Look at the definitions again and think in terms of your students. Have you had students who seemed to fit one definition better than another?
5. Have you developed a lesson or strategy you use with a guided reading group that you think improves fluency? Discuss it with your group.
6. What are your thoughts on the effectiveness of programs such as DEAR and USSR? How do your thoughts align with the NRP controversy?
7. Allington concludes this chapter with support for reading volume and its positive effect on fluency. What in your experience would support a positive or negative correlation between increased reading volume and improved fluency?
8. After reading this chapter, how would you rate the importance of fluency to reading proficiency? Is this the same as you felt before reading the chapter or has your thinking changed?

chapter 2: How Is Fluency Normally Developed?

1. What strategies from this chapter do you see yourself using? Why?

2. Generate a question this chapter caused you to wonder about. Bring it to the group for discussion.

3. Allington states that "most often children acquire the ability to read fluently, with phrasing and expression, with little guidance." Has this been true based on your experiences with most beginning readers?

4. Allington calls "voice-print matching, "understanding the concept of "word," and "attending to print" critical steps. Select a beginning struggling first-grade reader or even a fourth-, fifth-, or sixth-grader who is still at the beginning reading stage. As you work with him, watch carefully his eyes, noting if he actually is keeping his eyes on the print. Even if he is pointing to words, watch his eyes. Bring your observations to this group for discussion.

5. For students who don't attend to print, in addition to using a pointer, have you developed other techniques to help them acquire this skill?

6. What are some of the strategies you have found to be successful in helping students recognize function words?

7. Engage your students in a shared book experience every day for one week. Share your reactions and the reactions of your students with your book study group.

8. Try adapting the Oral Recitation Lesson framework with a passage from a content area text. Were you able to meet with some success or was the difficulty level of the text too inappropriate to make it work?

chapter 3: Why Do Some Readers Struggle with Fluency?

1. What strategies from this chapter do you see yourself using? Why?

2. Generate a question this chapter caused you to wonder about. Bring it to the group for discussion.

3. Make a list of the reading materials one of your struggling readers encounters each day. How many of these items do you think she can read at the 99% accuracy level?

4. Again look at your struggling readers who are receiving small-group or one-to-one intervention instruction. How many of those students are receiving the extra help in grade-level materials? How many are receiving that help in materials matched to their reading level?

5. Compare intervention instruction as well as classroom instruction for struggling readers from a fourth-, fifth-, or sixth-grade classroom to the instruction that struggling second-graders are receiving. Are more or less fourth-, fifth-, or sixth-graders receiving instruction in materials matched to their reading levels than second-graders? Are more or less fourth-, fifth-, or sixth-graders receiving instruction in grade-level materials than second-graders?

6. Determine how much of the time during your school day struggling readers spend actually engaged in high-success reading. In what percentile would that amount place them on Guthrie's scale?

7. What percentage of the goals of the instruction that struggling readers in your school receive is focused on developing decoding skills and what percentage is focused on increasing the volume of their high-success reading?

8. Consider lessons you have seen or taught in light of Allington's statements regarding what types of teacher behaviors are encountered by struggling readers versus those encountered by achieving readers. Do you find that what you know from watching teachers supports these differences?

chapter 4: How Should Fluency Be Assessed?

1. What strategies from this chapter do you see yourself using? Why?

2. Generate a question this chapter caused you to wonder about. Bring it to the group for discussion.

3. Consider Allington's arguments against the use of DIBELS as an assessment of fluency and discuss your thoughts on this assessment.

4. Create a chart. Put Allington's questions to ask yourself about why a student is having fluency problems down the side and your struggling readers' names across the top. Then put a +, –, or +/– by each question for each student. This chart will help you diagnose why the student might be struggling with fluency.

5. If you are using running records, describe any modifications you might have made in the procedure that have helped you get the best insight as to the instructional needs of your students.

6. Compare the results of running records for your students on reading cold versus reading previously read text. Which method do you think provided you with the best information about your students?

7. If you haven't previously tried some of the other assessments Allington describes, select two options to administer to your students and discuss their value in helping to improve instruction.

8. Determine which combination of assessments and how often you would administer each one to your struggling readers in order to best assess their fluency development.

chapter 5: Fostering the Development of Fluent Readers in Core Reading Lessons

1. What strategies from this chapter do you see yourself using? Why?

2. Generate a question this chapter caused you to wonder about. Bring it to the group for discussion.

3. Use a lesson from one of your core texts and modify it for fluency development by adding a shared book experience.

4. Use a lesson from one of your core texts and modify it for fluency development by adding a fluency development lesson.

5. Given your results from the lessons in items 3 and 4 above, which modification worked best for you and your students?

6. Tape (video or audio) yourself during a lesson with one of your struggling readers. Determine if Allington's "pause-prompt-praise" strategy is something that might be important for you to use.

7. Do you use reader's theater or some other type of repeated reading activity with your students? Have you adapted them in any way to improve their effectiveness with your students? Discuss your adaptations with the group.

8. Take each of Allington's four critical features of classrooms designed to foster free, voluntary reading and discuss what you might do to begin to improve these features in your classroom.

chapter 6: Interventions to Foster Fluency Development in Struggling Readers

1. What strategies from this chapter do you see yourself using? Why?

2. Generate a question this chapter caused you to wonder about. Bring it to the group for discussion.

3. Modify a repeated reading lesson you have used in the past or create a new lesson following Allington's guidelines for designing repeated reading lessons. Share your lesson with your group.

4. Teach your students to use the Tape-Check-Chart lesson design. Discuss with your group what you see as pros or cons of this strategy.

5. Identify which facets of your present reading program are most likely to foster teacher-directed reading lessons that include substantial amounts of reading activity and free, voluntary reading outside the intervention period.

6. Identify which facets of your present reading program are most likely to hinder teacher-directed reading lessons that include substantial amounts of reading activity and free, voluntary reading outside the intervention period.

7. With a story from your core reading program, use some of the activities Allington suggests to develop a lesson that focuses on "at-a-glance" words.

8. What do you believe is the most critical change that needs to be made in your school's reading program in order to improve the fluency of struggling readers? How might you begin to make that change?

Reading Reaction Sheet

Facilitator/Recorder (person who initiated the discussion): _____

Group reactants: _____

_____

Date of reaction/discussion: _____

Chapter title and author(s): _____

_____

Question #1: What ideas and information from this chapter could be used in classroom instruction?

Reactions:

Question #2: _____

_____

Reactions:

Question #3: _____

_____

Reactions:

Question #4: _____

_____

Reactions:

Bibliography

Adams, M. J. (1990). *Beginning to read: Thinking and learning about print.* Cambridge, MA: MIT Press.

Allington, R. L. (1977). If they don't read much, how they ever gonna get good? *Journal of Reading, 21,* 57–61.

Allington, R. L. (1980). Teacher interruption behaviors during primary grade oral reading. *Journal of Educational Psychology, 72,* 371–377.

Allington, R. L. (1983a). Fluency: The neglected goal. *Reading Teacher, 36,* 556–561.

Allington, R. L. (1983b). The reading instruction provided readers of differing abilities. *Elementary School Journal, 83,* 548–559.

Allington, R. L. (1984). Content coverage and contextual reading in reading groups. *Journal of Reading Behavior, 16*(1), 85–96.

Allington, R. L. (2002). Research on reading/learning disability interventions. In A. E. Farstrup & S. J. Samuels (Eds.), *What research says about reading instruction* (3rd ed., pp. 261–290). Newark, DE: International Reading Association.

Allington, R. L. (2006a). Fluency: Still waiting after all these years. In S. J. Samuels & A. Farstrup (Eds.), *What research has to say about fluency instruction* (pp. 94–105). Newark, DE: International Reading Association.

Allington, R. L. (2006b). *What really matters for struggling readers: Designing research-based programs* (2nd ed.). Boston: Allyn & Bacon.

Allington, R. L. (2007a). Fluency as an instructional problem. *Teachers College Record.* On-line publication, available at www.tcrecord.org (ID no. 13585).

Allington, R. L. (2007b). Intervention all day long: New hope for struggling readers. *Voices from the Middle, 14*(4), 7–14.

Allington, R. L. (in press). *If they don't read much . . . : Thirty years later.* In E. H. Hiebert (Ed.), *Reading more, reading better.* Newark, DE: International Reading Association.

Allington, R. L., & Brown, S. (1979). *Fact: A multimedia reading program.* Milwaukee, WI: Raintree Publishers.

Allington, R. L., & McGill-Franzen, A. (1989). Different programs, indifferent instruction. In A. Gartner & D. Lipsky (Eds.), *Beyond separate education: Quality education for all* (pp. 75–98). Baltimore: Brookes.

Allington, R. L., McGill-Franzen, A. M., Camilli, G., Williams, L., Graff, J., Zeig, J., Zmach, C., & Nowak, R. (2007). *Ameliorating summer reading setback among economically disadvantaged elementary students.* Paper presented at the American Educational Research Association, Chicago.

Altwerger, B., Jordan, N., & Shelton, N. R. (2008). *Rereading fluency: Process, practice, and policies.* Portsmouth, NH: Heinemann.

Anderson, R. C., Wilson, P., & Fielding, L. (1988). Growth in reading and how children spend their time outside of school. *Reading Research Quarterly, 23,* 285–303.

Armbruster, B., Lehr, F., & Osborn, J. (2001). *Put reading first.* Washington, DC: National Institute for Literacy.

Beach, J. D. (2006, November 18). *Why don't children read children's literature?* Paper presented at the National Council of Teachers of English, Nashville, TN.

Biemiller, A. (1970). The development of the use of graphic and contextual information as children learn to read. *Reading Research Quarterly, 6*(1), 75–96.

Brownstein, A., & Hicks, T. (2006). Ed ignored early warnings on reading first conflicts, report says: Officials obscure origins of influential assessment review. *Title 1 Monitor, 11*(11), 1–4, 17–21.

Buly, M. R., & Valencia, S. W. (2002). Below the bar: Profiles of students who fail state reading assessments. *Educational Evaluation and Policy Analysis, 24*(3), 219–239.

Chall, J. S. (1983). *Stages of reading development*. New York: McGraw-Hill.

Chinn, C. A., Waggoner, M. A., Anderson, R. C., Schommer, M., & Wilkinson, I. (1993). Situated actions during reading lessons: A microanalysis of oral reading error episodes. *American Educational Research Journal, 30*, 361–392.

Clay, M. M. (1969). Reading errors and self-correction behaviour. *British Journal of Educational Psychology, 37*, 47–56.

Clay, M. M. (1985). *The early detection of reading difficulties: A diagnostic survey with recovering procedures* (3rd ed.). Exeter, NH: Heinemann.

Connor, C. M., Morrison, F. J., Fishman, B. J., Schatschneider, C., & Underwood, P. (2007, January). Algorithm-guided individualized reading instruction. *Science, 315*, 464–465.

Connor, C. M., Morrison, F. J., & Katch, E. L. (2004). Beyond the reading wars: The effect of classroom instruction by child interactions on early reading. *Scientific Studies of Reading, 8*, 305–336.

Cunningham, A. E., & Stanovich, K. E. (1998). The impact of print exposure on word recognition. In J. Metsala & L. Ehri (Eds.), *Word recognition in beginning literacy* (pp. 235–262). Mahwah, NJ: Erlbaum.

Cunningham, P. M. (2004). *Phonics they use: Words for reading and writing* (3rd ed.). New York: Longmans.

Cunningham, P. M., & Allington, R. L. (2007). *Classrooms that work: They can all read and write* (4th ed.). Boston: Allyn & Bacon.

Daane, M. C., Campbell, J. R., Grigg, W. S., Goodman, M. J., & Oranje, A. (2005). *Fourth-grade students reading aloud: NAEP 2002 special study of oral reading* (No. NCES 2006-469). Washington, DC: U.S. Department of Education, Institute of Education Sciences, National Center for Educational Statistics, Government Printing Office.

Dahl, P. R., & Samuels, S. J. (1977). An experimental program for teaching high-speed word recognition and comprehension skills. In J. Button, T. Lovitt, & T. Rowland (Eds.), *Communications research in learning disabilities and mental retardation* (pp. 33–65). Baltimore: University Park Press.

deJong, P. F., & Share, D. L. (2007). Orthographic learning during oral and silent reading. *Scientific Studies of Reading, 11*(1), 55–71.

Deno, S. (1985). Curriculum-based measurement: The emerging alternative. *Exceptional Children, 52*(3), 219–232.

Deno, S. L., & Marston, D. (2006). Curriculum-based measurement of oral reading: An indicator of growth in fluency. In S. J. Samuels & A. E. Farstrup (Eds.), *What research has to say about fluency instruction* (pp. 179–203). Newark, DE: International Reading Association.

Dolch, E. W. (1936). A basic sight vocabulary. *Elementary School Journal, 36*, 456–460.

Durrell, D. D. (1955). *Durrell Analysis of Reading Difficulties*. New York: Harcourt, Brace & World.

Dweck, C. S. (1986). Motivational processes affecting learning. *American Psychologist, 41*, 1040–1048.

Eder, D., & Felmlee, D. (1984). The development of attention norms in ability groups. In P. L. Peterson, L. C. Wilkinson, & M. Hallinan (Eds.), *The social context of instruction: Group organization and group process*. New York: Academic Press.

Ehri, L. C., Dreyer, L. G., Flugman, B., & Gross, A. (2007). Reading rescue: An effective tutoring intervention model for language-minority students who are struggling readers in first grade. *American Educational Research Journal, 44*(2), 414–448.

Eldredge, J. L., Reutzel, D. R., & Hollingsworth, P. M. (1996). Comparing the effectiveness of two oral reading practices: Round-robin reading and shared book experience. *Journal of Literacy Research, 28*(2), 201–226.

Ericsson, K. A., Krampe, R. T., & Tesch Romer, C. (1993). The role of deliberate practice in the acquisition of expert performance. *Psychological Review, 100*(3), 363–406.

Fielding, L. G., Wilson, P. T., & Anderson, R. C. (1986). A new focus on free reading: The role of trade books in reading instruction. In T. E. Raphael (Ed.), *The contexts of school-based literacy* (pp. 149–160). New York: Random House.

Fink, R. (2006). *Why Jane and Johnny couldn't read—And how they learned*. Newark, DE: International Reading Association.

Fuchs, L. S., Deno, S. L., & Mirkin, P. K. (1984). Effects of frequent curriculum-based measurement on pedagogy, student achievement, and student awareness of learning. *American Educational Research Journal, 21*, 449–460.

Gambrell, L. B., Palmer, B., Codling, R. M., & Mazzoni, S. A. (1996). Assessing motivation to read. *Reading Teacher, 49*, 518–533.

Gambrell, L. B., Wilson, R. M., & Gantt, W. N. (1981). Classroom observations of task-attending behaviors of good and poor readers. *Journal of Educational Research, 74*(6), 400–404.

Gaskins, I. W. (2005). *Success with struggling readers: The Benchmark School approach.* New York: Guilford.

Glenn, D. (2007, February 2). Reading for profit: Whistle-blowers allege that U. of Oregon scholars steered bounty from the No Child Left Behind Act to themselves and their colleagues. *Chronicle of Higher Education,* p. A8.

Good, R. H., & Kaminski, R. A. (2002). *Dynamic indicators of basic early literacy skills* (6th ed.). Retrieved December 13, 2002, from http://dibels.uoregon.edu.

Goodman, K. (2006). *A critical review of DIBELS: What it is, what it does.* Portsmouth, NH: Heinemann.

Griffith, L. W., & Rasinski, T. V. (2004). A focus on fluency: How one teacher incorporated fluency in her reading curriculum. *Reading Teacher, 58*, 126–137.

Guthrie, J. T. (2004). Teaching for literacy engagement. *Journal of Literacy Research, 36*(1), 1–28.

Guthrie, J. T., & Humenick, N. M. (2004). Motivating students to read: Evidence for classroom practices that increase motivation and achievement. In P. McCardle & V. Chhabra (Eds.), *The voice of evidence in reading research* (pp. 329–354). Baltimore: Brookes.

Hasbrouck, J., & Tindal, G. A. (2006). ORF norms: A valuable assessment tool for reading teachers. *Reading Teacher, 59*(7), 636–644.

Hasselbring, T. S., & Goin, L. I. (2004). Literacy instruction for older struggling readers: What is the role of technology? *Reading & Writing Quarterly, 20,* 123–144.

Hiebert, E. H. (1983). An examination of ability grouping for reading instruction. *Reading Research Quarterly, 18,* 231–255.

Hiebert, E. H. (2002). Becoming fluent: What difference do texts make? In S. J. Samuels & A. E. Farstrup (Eds.), *What research has to say about reading fluency* (pp. 204–226). Newark, DE: International Reading Association.

Hiebert, E. H., & Fisher, C. W. (2005). A review of the National Reading Panel's studies on fluency: The role of text. *Elementary School Journal, 105*(5), 443–460.

Hoffman, J. V., O'Neal, S., Kastler, L., Clements, R., Segel, K., & Nash, M. F. (1984). Guided oral reading and miscue focused verbal feedback in second-grade classrooms. *Reading Research Quarterly, 19,* 367–384.

Hoffman, J. V., Roser, N. L., & Battle, J. (1993, March). Reading aloud in classrooms: From modal to a model. *Reading Teacher, 46*(6), 496–505.

Homan, S., Klesius, P., & Hite, S. (1993). Effects of repeated readings and nonrepetitive strategies on students' fluency and comprehension. *Journal of Educational Research, 87*(1), 94–99.

Huey, E. B. (1908/1968). *The psychology and pedagogy of reading.* New York: Macmillan.

Jachym, N., Allington, R. L., & Broikou, K. A. (1989). Estimating the cost of seatwork. *Reading Teacher, 43*(1), 30–37.

Johnston, P. (1991). *Constructive evaluation of literate activity.* New York: Longmans.

Johnston, P. (2000). *Running records.* York, ME: Stenhouse.

Johnston, P., & Winograd, P. (1985). Passive failure in reading. *Journal of Reading Behavior, 17,* 279–301.

Jorgenson, G. W. (1977). Relationship of classroom behavior to the accuracy of the match between material difficulty and student ability. *Journal of Educational Psychology, 69*(1), 24–32.

Kameenui, E. J., & Simmons, D. C. (2001). The DNA of reading fluency. *Scientific Studies of Reading, 5*(3), 203–210.

Kaplan, A. G. (2007). Is your school librarian "highly qualified"? *Phi Delta Kappan, 89*(4), 300–303.

Knapp, M. S. (1995). *Teaching for meaning in high-poverty classrooms.* New York: Teachers College Press.

Krashen, S. (2003). The (lack of) experimental evidence supporting the use of Accelerated Reader. *Journal of Children's Literature, 29*(2), 16–30.

Krashen, S. (2004). *The power of reading: Insights from the research* (2nd ed.). Portsmouth, NH: Heinemann.

Kuhn, M. R. (2005a). A comparative study of small group fluency instruction. *Reading Psychology, 26,* 127–146.

Kuhn, M. R. (2005b). Helping students become accurate, expressive readers: Fluency instruction for small groups. *Reading Teacher, 58*(4), 338–344.

Kuhn, M. R., Schwanenflugel, P., Morris, R. D., Morrow, L. M., Woo, D., Meisinger, B., et al. (2006). Teaching children to become fluent and automatic readers. *Journal of Literacy Research, 38*(4), 357–388.

Kuhn, M. R., & Stahl, S. A. (1998). Teaching children to learn word meanings from context: A synthesis and some questions. *Journal of Literacy Research, 30*(1), 119–138.

Kuhn, M. R., & Stahl, S. A. (2003). Fluency: A review of developmental and remedial practices. *Journal of Educational Psychology, 95*(1), 3–21.

LaBerge, D., & Samuels, S. J. (1974). Toward a theory of automatic information processing in reading. *Cognitive Psychology, 6*, 293–323.

Lamme, L., Fu, D., & Allington, R. (2002). "Is this book an AR book?" A closer examination of a popular reading program. *Florida Reading Quarterly, 38*(3), 27–32.

Lewis, M., & Samuels, S. J. (2004). *Read more, read better? A meta-analysis of the literature on the relationship between exposure to reading and reading achievement.* Unpublished paper, Minneapolis, University of Minnesota.

Lyon, G. R., & Moats, L. C. (1997). Critical conceptual and methodological considerations in reading intervention research. *Journal of Learning Disabilities, 30*(6), 578–588.

Markell, M. A., & Deno, S. L. (1997). Effects of increasing oral reading: Generalizations across tasks. *Journal of Special Education, 31*(2), 233–245.

Martinez, M. G., Roser, N. L., & Strecker, S. K. (1999). "I never thought I could be a star": A reader's theater ticket to fluency. *Reading Teacher, 54*(4), 326–335.

Mathson, D., Solic, K., & Allington, R. L. (2006). Hijacking fluency and instructionally informative assessment. In T. Rasinski, C. Blachowicz, & K. Lems (Eds.), *Fluency instruction:Research-based best practice* (pp. 106–119). New York: Guilford.

McGill-Franzen, A. (1993). "I could read the words!" Selecting good books for inexperienced readers. *Reading Teacher, 46*(6), 424–426.

McGill-Franzen, A. (2006). *Kindergarten literacy.* New York: Scholastic.

McGill-Franzen, A., & Allington, R. L. (1990). Comprehension and coherence: Neglected elements of literacy instruction in remedial and resource room services. *Journal of Reading and Writing, 6*(2), 149–182.

McGill-Franzen, A., & McDermott, P. (1978, December). *Negotiating a reading diagnosis.* Paper presented at the National Reading Conference, St. Petersburg, FL.

McGill-Franzen, A., Zmach, C., Solic, K., & Zeig, J. L. (2006). The confluence of two policy mandates: Core reading programs and third-grade retention in Florida. *Elementary School Journal, 107*(1), 67–91.

McIntyre, E., Rightmeyer, E., Powell, R., Powers, S., & Petrosko, J. (2006). How much should young children read? A study of the relationship between development and instruction. *Literacy Teaching and Learning, 11*(1), 51–72.

Meyer, L. M., & Wardrop, J. L. (1994). Home and school influences on learning to read in kindergarten through second grade. In F. Lehr & J. Osborn (Eds.), *Reading, language, and literacy: Instruction for the twenty-first century* (pp. 165–184). Hillsdale, NJ: Erlbaum.

Morrow, L. M., & Weinstein, C. S. (1986). Encouraging voluntary reading: The impact of a literature program on children's use of library centers. *Reading Research Quarterly, 21*, 330–346.

National Reading Panel. (2000). *Teaching children to read: An evidence-based assessment of the scientific research literature on reading and its implications for reading instruction.* www.nationalreadingpanel.org.

Nicholson, T., & Tan, A. (1999). Proficient word identification for comprehension. In G. B. Thompson & T. Nicholson (Eds.), *Learning to read: Beyond phonics and whole language* (pp. 150–173). New York: Teachers College Press.

Nunnery, J. A., Ross, S. M., & McDonald, A. (2006). A randomized experimental evaluation of the impact of accelerated reader/reading renaissance implementation on reading achievement in grades 3 to 6. *Journal of Education for Students Placed at Risk, 11*(1), 1–18.

Nye, B., Konstantopoulos, S., & Hedges, L. V. (2004). How large are teacher effects? *Educational Evaluation and Policy Analysis, 26*, 237–257.

O'Connor, R. E., Bell, K. M., Harty, K. R., Larkin, L. K., Sackor, S. M., & Zigmond, N. (2002). Teaching reading to poor readers in the intermediate grades: A comparison of text difficulty. *Journal of Educational Psychology, 94*(3), 474–485.

Office of the Inspector General. (2006). *The Reading First program's grant application process: Final inspection report* (No. ED-OIG/I13-F0017). Washington, DC: U.S. Department of Education.

Pavonetti, L., Brimmer, K., & Cipielewski, J. (2003). Accelerated reader: What are the lasting effects on the reading habits of middle school students exposed to accelerated reader in elementary grades? *Journal of Adolescent and Adult Literacy, 46*(4), 300–311.

Pinnell, G. S., Pikulski, J. J., Wixson, K., Campbell, J. R., Gough, P. B., & Beatty, A. S. (1995). *Listening to children read aloud.* (Research report No. ED 378550). Washington, DC: National Center for Educational Statistics.

Pressley, M., Hilden, K., & Shankland, R. (2005). *An evaluation of end-of-grade 3 Dynamic Indicators of Basic Early Literacy Skills (DIBELS): Speed reading without comprehension, predicting little.* East Lansing: Literacy Achievement Research Center, Michigan State University.

Pressley, M., Wharton-McDonald, R., Allington, R. L., Block, C. C., Morrow, L., Tracey, D., et al. (2001). A study of effective first-grade literacy instruction. *Scientific Studies in Reading, 5*(1), 35–58.

Rashotte, C., & Torgeson, J. (1985). Repeated readings and reading fluency in learning disabled children. *Reading Research Quarterly, 20*, 180–189.

Rasinski, T. V., & Hoffman, J. V. (2003). Oral reading in the school literacy curriculum. *Reading Research Quarterly, 38*(4), 510–523.

Reutzel, D. R., Eldredge, J. L., & Hollingsworth, P. M. (1994). Oral reading instruction: The impact on student reading development. *Reading Research Quarterly, 29*(1), 40–65.

Reutzel, D. R., & Hollingsworth, P. M. (1993). Effects of fluency training on second graders' reading comprehension. *Journal of Educational Research, 86*(6), 325–331.

Ross, J. A. (2004). Effects of running records assessment on early literacy achievement. *Journal of Educational Research, 97*(2), 186–195.

Rylant, C. (2000). *Henry and Mudge and Annie's perfect pet.* New York: Aladdin.

Samuels, S. J. (1979). The method of repeated reading. *Reading Teacher, 32*, 403–408.

Samuels, S. J. (2002). Reading fluency: Its development and assessment. In A. Farstrup & S. J. Samuels (Eds.), *What research has to say about reading instruction* (3rd ed., pp. 166–183). Newark, DE: International Reading Association.

Samuels, S. J. (2006). Toward a model of reading fluency. In S. J. Samuels & A. E. Farstrup (Eds.), *What research has to say about fluency instruction* (pp. 24–46). Newark, DE: International Reading Association.

Samuels, S. J. (2007). The DIBELS tests: Is speed of barking at print what we mean by reading fluency, or comprehension for that matter? *Reading Research Quarterly, 42*(4), 563–566.

Samuels, S. J., & Wu, Y. C. (2003). *How the amount of time spent on reading affects reading achievement: A response to the National Reading Panel.* Minneapolis: University of Minnesota.

Scanlon, D. M., Vellutino, F. R., Small, S. G., Fanuele, D. P., & Sweeney, J. M. (2005). Severe reading difficulties—Can they be prevented? A comparison of prevention and intervention approaches. *Exceptionality, 13*(4), 209–227.

Schilling, S. G., Carlisle, J. F., Scott, S. E., & Zeng, J. (2007). Are fluency measures accurate predictors of reading achievement? *Elementary School Journal, 107*(5), 429–448.

Shanahan, T. (2002, May 22). Reading report's unending debate. *Education Week,* p. 38.

Share, D. L. (1995). Phonological recoding and self-teaching: Sine qua non of reading acquisition. *Cognition, 55*, 151–218.

Share, D. L., & Stanovich, K. E. (1995). Cognitive processes in early reading development: Accommodating individual differences in a model of acquisition. *Issues in Education, 1*(1), 1–57.

Shin, F. H., & Krashen, S. D. (2008). *Summer reading: Program and evidence.* Boston: Allyn & Bacon.

Shinn, M. (1989). *Curriculum-based assessment: Assessing special children.* New York: Guilford.

Smith, D. D. (1979). The improvement of children's oral reading through the use of teacher modeling. *Journal of Learning Disabilities, 12*(1), 39–42.

Smith, N. B. (1925). *One thousand ways to teach silent reading.* Yonkers, NY: World Book Co.

Smith, N. B. (1934). *American reading instruction.* New York: Silver Burdette and Co., revised and reissued by the International Reading Association, 1965.

Snow, C. E., Burns, M. S., & Griffin, P. (1998). *Preventing reading difficulties in young children: A report of the National Research Council.* Washington, DC: National Academy Press.

Stahl, S. A. (1999). *Vocabulary development: From reading research to practice.* Newton Upper Falls, MA: Brookline.

Stahl, S. A., & Heubach, K. M. (2005). Fluency-oriented reading instruction. *Journal of Literacy Research, 37*(1), 25–60.

Stanovich, K. E. (2000). *Progress in understanding reading: Scientific foundations and new frontiers.* New York: Guilford.

Stanovich, K. E., & West, R. (1989). Exposure to print and orthographic processing. *Reading Research Quarterly, 26,* 402–429.

Stanovich, K. E., West, R. F., Cunningham, A. E., Cipielewski, J., & Siddiqui, S. (1996). The role of inadequate print exposure as a determinate of reading comprehension problems. In C. Cornoldi & J. Oakhill (Eds.), *Reading comprehension difficulties: Processes and intervention* (pp. 15–32). Mahwah, NJ: Erlbaum.

Stayter, F., & Allington, R. L. (1991). Fluency and comprehension of texts. *Theory into Practice, 33*(3), 143–148.

Therrien, W. J. (2003). Fluency and comprehension gains as a result of repeated reading: A meta-analysis. *Remedial and Special Education, 25*(4), 252–261.

Torgeson, J. K., & Hudson, R. F. (2006). Reading fluency: Critical issues for struggling readers. In S. J. Samuels & A. E. Farstrup (Eds.), *What research has to say about fluency instruction* (pp. 130–158). Newark, DE: International Reading Association.

Trelease, J. (2001). *Read-aloud handbook* (5th ed.). New York: Viking-Penguin.

Vadasy, P. F., Sanders, E. A., & Peyton, J. A. (2005). Relative effectiveness of reading practice or word-level instruction in supplemental tutoring: How text matters. *Journal of Learning Disabilities, 38*(4), 364–380.

Vaughn, S., Moody, S., & Schumm, J. S. (1998). Broken promises: Reading instruction in the resource room. *Exceptional Children, 64*(3), 211–225.

Vaughn, S., Linan-Thompson, S., Kouzekanani, K., Bryant, D. P., Dickson, S., & Blozis, S. A. (2003). Reading instruction grouping for students with reading difficulties. *Remedial and Special Education, 24*(5), 301–315.

Vellutino, F. R. (2003). Individual differences as sources of variability in reading comprehension in elementary school children. In A. P. Sweet & C. E. Snow (Eds.), *Rethinking reading comprehension* (pp. 51–81). New York: Guilford.

Walczyk, J. A., & Griffith-Ross, D. A. (2007). How important is reading skill fluency for comprehension? *Reading Teacher, 60*(6), 560–569.

Weber, R. M. (1970). A linguistic analysis of first grade reading errors. *Reading Research Quarterly, 5,* 427–451.

Weber, R. M. (2006). Function words in the prosody of fluent reading. *Journal of Research in Reading, 29*(3), 258–269.

Weber, R. M. (2008). The shape of direct quotation. *Reading Teacher, 61*(6).

Wilde, S. (2006). But isn't DIBELS scientifically based? In K. Goodman (Ed.), *The truth about DIBELS: What it is—What it does* (pp. 66–70). Portsmouth, NH: Heinemann.

Worthy, J., Broaddus, K., & Ivey, G. (2001). *Pathways to independence: Reading, writing, and learning in grades 3–8.* New York: Guilford.

Worthy, J., & Prater, K. (2002). "I thought about it all night": Reader's theater for reading fluency and motivation. *Reading Teacher, 56,* 294–297.

Index